Preaching and
the New Reformation

Preaching AND
THE New Reformation

The Lyman Beecher Lectures

By TRUMAN B. DOUGLASS

HARPER & BROTHERS   PUBLISHERS   NEW YORK

Library of Congress catalog card number: 56–7032

For Virginia

Contents

FOREWORD   ix

I. RESOURCE AND COMMAND   1

II. THE RENEWING WORD   17

III. THE WORD OF THE CHURCH   37

IV. THE CATHOLIC WORD   57

V. THE COMMUNICABLE WORD   91

VI. PREACHING THE REFORMATION   111

NOTES   133

INDEX   139

Foreword

Whoever attempts to interpret any phase of the Ecumenical Movement is promptly involved in the Heraclitean predicament. He can never dip twice into the same stream, for the waters continually flow on and leave him beside a different river.

In the course of preparing and revising these lectures I have been made sharply aware that whatever else the Ecumenical Movement may or may not be it is indubitably—and embarrassingly—a *movement!* When I have consulted with members of the staff of the World Council of Churches and with others, they have more than once said, "It's a pity that your book cannot be delayed until next year, or the year after; by that time a comprehensive report on this subject, now in the hands of a study committee, will be available." I have comforted myself with the thought that next year, or the year after, I should probably hear the same story.

Between the First Assembly of the World Council of Churches at Amsterdam, the official report of which had just been published when I began work on these lectures, and the Second Assembly at Evanston, the report of which has been at hand during the final revision of the manuscript, events in the ecumenical world have moved swiftly.

In addition to the World Council assemblies, highly important meetings have been held under the auspices of the Faith and Order Commission and the International Missionary Council. Studies preparatory to these meetings and reports of their proceedings have become significant items in the literature of modern ecumenicity. Numerous plans for unions of churches have been actively pursued. Though some, unhappily, have been postponed or even abandoned, others have been or are about to be consummated.

Still more important is the penetration of ecumenical interests into the consciousness of millions of persons, both within and without the churches. When one contrasts the extraordinary press coverage of the Evanston meetings with the journalistic silence that surrounded the Oxford and Edinburgh conferences only thirty years previous, this gain in popular awareness is impressive indeed.

If for no other reason than that it is so widely known and discussed, to a considerable extent even in lay circles, the Ecumenical Movement is now a fact to be taken into account by the preacher. That it is not only an inevitable subject of preaching but is also both a resource and objective of the preacher as he seeks to articulate the Christian message, is the thesis I have tried to develop in these chapters.

It may be well at the outset to warn the reader of a certain practical bias and method of approach which have been brought to a subject that sometimes appears to be left pretty largely to the theoreticians. Not that I am condescending toward questions of theory; indeed, I have come to see the fundamental importance of the theological and doctrinal issues involved. Some of us can agree with Karl Barth at least to the point of saying with him: "From the children's disease of being ashamed of theology I think I have to some degree recovered." [1] This recovery, in my own case, has followed rather than preceded a concern for the practical implications of ecumenicity. My own interest in the Ecumenical Movement, I think it is fair to say, has been primarily pastoral and homiletical. I should like to think that "evangelical" may be the proper word. It is this fact that gives me hope of calling attention to some of the meanings of this movement for parish ministers and preachers.

When T. S. Eliot was asked to contribute to a symposium on the subject of "Revelation," he introduced his essay by remarking that the invitation must have been extended to him because, as he was not a theologian, the editor presumed that he had, as Eliot put it, "an intimate and affectionate acquaintance with the limbo and lower regions in which the secular world moves; a knowledge of objects towards which the theological mind is not often directed." "My qualification," said Eliot, "is the eye of the owl, not that of the eagle." [2]

In a lesser way, that is perhaps my equipment and excuse for trespassing on these precincts. Mine is the owl's-eye view; I have been a bird of the ecumenical night. In the regions where the theological eagles soar the light is too strong for my gaze. But in the twilight and gloom far below, where I reside, I have at least seen something of the appalling and predatory business that goes on where ecumenicity is wanting.

A second peculiarity of my case is the largely informal character of my acquaintance with the organized Ecumenical Movement. If attendance at world conferences on one thing or another is a necessary qualification for discussing this subject, I am out of my field. I am not one of the ecumenical Rover Boys—the lads who at the sound of rustling agenda are off for Geneva, Madras, Bangkok, or some other distant point to attend a meeting of a study commission, a continuing committee, or some similar organized body. I belong to the select and diminishing company of ministers over forty years of age who have never attended a world conference on anything.* It may be a rationalization of this stay-at-home attitude, but I have come to believe that the most fruitful work of the Ecumenical Movement is being done outside these formal gatherings. The meetings are necessary, I am sure, and they have frequently provided the incentive and starting point for this more valuable work. But the results of the meetings are available to those of us who cannot afford an airplane ticket to Geneva. More positively, I believe that the Ecumenical Movement must be got outside the assembly halls and committee rooms into the life of parish and pulpit if it is to be more than the vocation of a coterie of specialists. The desire to speak for this liberation and dissemination is one of the motives impelling me toward this subject. If for no other reason than that it is so widely known and discussed, the Ecumenical Movement is now a fact to be taken into account by the preacher. That it is not only an inevitable subject of preaching but is also both a resource and an objective of the preacher's message in our time, is the thesis I have tried to develop in these chapters.

* This is still true, though I was elected an official delegate to Evanston. Illness prevented my attendance, and thus saved my amateur standing.

My obligations of gratitude are too numerous to catalog, and I mention only the persons who have helped me most directly. To Dean Liston Pope and the Faculty of the Yale University Divinity School I am deeply grateful for the invitation to give the Lyman Beecher Lectures, and for their generosity in allowing me to explore a theme somewhat outside the range of subjects ordinarily associated with this lectureship. Toward Professor and Mrs. Halford E. Luccock, my wife and I feel a special warmth of appreciation for their many personal kindnesses to us during our stay in New Haven. The Rev. Robert S. Bilheimer, Secretary of the Study Department of the World Council of Churches, made available several important documents before publication, among them the reports on *Intercommunion*, on *Ways of Worship*, and on *The Nature of the Church* preparatory to the Lund Conference on Faith and Order, and the manuscript of the book *Biblical Authority for Today*. To my friend the Rev. Daniel T. Jenkins, who extraordinarily combines the ministry of a Congregational church in England with a three months' annual teaching stint as Professor of Ecumenical Theology at the University of Chicago, I acknowledge an obligation even greater than is indicated by the extensive citations from his writings. He is one of the few persons engaged in thinking in a systematic and sustained way about the central issues of ecumenicity. Without making him in the slightest degree responsible for any of the judgments put forth in this book, I express my gratitude for the help I have received in the course of numerous conversations with him.

I am grateful to the Directors of the Board of Home Missions of the Congregational Christian Churches, who allowed me a two months' leave of absence from my administrative duties; and to our cousins, Mr. and Mrs. Charles Krampf, whose loan of their charming house in South Carolina permitted me to do much of the writing under the most pleasant circumstances imaginable.

To the late John B. Chambers of Harper & Brothers, whose untimely death deprived his firm and a group of authors who greatly relied on him of an uncommonly sensitive and skillful editor, I feel a special indebtedness for numerous suggestions, nearly all of which I have tried to follow.

My secretary, Miss Dorothy Bayer, has given her extraordinary diligence and skill to the typing and retyping of the manuscript and to the preparation of the index. To my wife, who continued to believe, despite all evidence to the contrary, that I would one day actually reduce these lectures to writing, I give thanks for her patience and faith.

TRUMAN B. DOUGLASS

Preaching and
the New Reformation

. . . the present church situation is characterized by the progress of a profound reformation. . . . This reformation is the ecumenical reformation. It is in process now and has been for perhaps as much as a century. . . . Though it has its influential leaders, it differs from the Protestant Reformation in that it has not been set in motion primarily by the leadership of great prophets. The historian of the ecumenical movement cannot look back upon one or two, as Protestants turn back to Luther and Calvin. The ecumenical reformation is the result rather of multitudinous voices and efforts, some of them organized and some of them unorganized, some of them conscious of the reform they were seeking and some wholly unconscious of it. In spite, however, of the length of its duration and its lack of decisive and towering prophets, its vigor and its importance for the Church should not be underestimated. Indeed, it may be just because of the implications of the slow tempo of its progress and the widespread nature of its leadership that it may be the most profound and far-reaching of the reformations which the Church has yet undergone. . . .

It is reformation which amid the disunity of the churches asserts the unity of the Church. It is a reformation which amid the provincialism of the churches asserts the world mission of the Church. It is a reformation born of the desires of a multitude of people, of a hundred different types of organized effort and in response to the spontaneous prayer of persons in all lands and churches.

ROBERT S. BILHEIMER [1]

The quickening of faith and obedience among Christ's people has often in the past been independent of church authorities and institutions, and impatient with their tendency to petrifaction. But for half a century there has been a stirring of dry bones among ecclesiastics, and what is probably the greatest tide of religious renewal in our day has caught up the leaders of the churches in a fresh impulse to witness in unity to the world of the mercies they have received.

JAMES HASTINGS NICHOLS [2]

CHAPTER I

Resource and Command

RECKONED by what is now a widely accepted method of dating, the modern Ecumenical Movement is only a little more than forty years old. Yet in the course of these four swift decades it has assumed the dimensions and significance of a major reformation of the Church.[3] In this brief period it has also taken on an increasingly self-aware and coherent character. It has produced a large and rapidly growing literature; formed organizational and institutional organs of expression and continuity; and called to its service a company of leaders who, though not wielding the individual influence of the sixteenth-century reformers, are persons of competence and distinction, recognized as belonging to this movement and as speaking for it in a deeply responsible way. It has devised a technical—and for the layman a somewhat formidable—vocabulary. Terms such as "faith and order," "life and work," "the Lambeth quadrilateral," "intercommunion," "corporate union," and of course the word "ecumenical" itself, have taken on specific content and meaning for those who have learned to discourse in this realm. To those who have participated in the life and thought of this movement has been granted, if not a "catholic mind," at least some intimation of what Richard Niebuhr has called "The Gift of Catholic Vision"; [4] and there is today a world-wide company of Christians who feel themselves brought together in a special way by the imperative of this vision. No informed person can doubt that this Ecumenical Movement exists, that it has identity and substance.

The implications and consequences of this movement for the work of the preacher of the Gospel are the subjects to which this discussion is addressed. What does it mean to be a preacher of the Word in a day when the irrepressible longing for the unity of the Church is finding new clarity and passion of utterance? What does it mean to be concerned for the communication of the Christian faith in a generation when every traditional form in which it has come to us is to be proclaimed with a new humility, recognizing the mutilated character of all these forms, and at the same time recognizing that all of them have their place somewhere in the total confessional life of the Christian Community across the ages? How is the vocation of the preacher affected by the fact that no literate minister today can address himself to his work as if the ecumenical reality and spirit did not exist? What has this new catholicity given to us as preachers, and what are we as preachers called of God to do with that gift?

Our consideration will deal with the *interaction* between the Ecumenical Movement and the preacher, for it is evident that a reciprocal process is at work. This movement at once influences our preaching and is being influenced by it. On the one side the ecumenical Church—which in some real though not easily definable sense is already in being today—preaches *through* us. If we preachers have any acquaintance with it at all, it colors, enriches, qualifies, reinforces, and in some measure regulates the content of our message. We cannot preach the Christian Gospel as if this encounter with the ecumenical Church had not taken place and had not told us something about what the Church's message is. On the other side, we are called to be preachers *of* this Church, believing boldly that we are called to preach it into fuller actualization. That may seem at first a prideful and impious statement. The unity of the Church, in the words of Amsterdam, is God's creation, not our achievement. Or, as Edinburgh 1937 put it:

Such a living community (as a united Church), like all that lives, cannot be a construction; life can come only from life; the visible unity of the Body of Christ can issue only from the living God through the work of the life-giving Spirit.[5]

How then can we dare to speak of preaching the united Church into being? Yet, if preaching is in God's purpose one of the "constitutive acts" of the Church—that is, one of the acts by which the

Church comes into being and which is requisite to the existence of any Church at all—then even our faltering service of the Word may become one of the means by which the great Church is more fully constituted. The ecumenical Church is thus both a source and a goal of the preacher's message.

That there exists a vital reciprocity between the Ecumenical Movement and preaching may well be one of those surprises with which the record of the New Reformation is replete. The story of the past forty years is one of outcomes surpassing intentions, of results exceeding all the calculated and agreed-upon plans of their human agents, of harvests which many a modern Apollos helped to water—but frequently under the impression that they were irrigating a quite different species of flora!

William Temple, in an oft-quoted passage from his enthronement sermon, spoke of "the great new fact of our era": the world-wide Christian fellowship.

No human agency has planned this. It is the result of the great missionary enterprise of the last hundred and fifty years. Neither the missionaries nor those who sent them out were aiming at the creation of a world-wide fellowship. . . . The aim for nearly the whole period was to preach the Gospel to as many individuals as could be reached. . . . Almost incidentally the great world fellowship has arisen; it is the great new fact of our era. . . .[6]

More recently we have been reminded by Oliver Tomkins, a secretary of the World Council of Churches, that the Ecumenical Movement itself came into being as an unintended consequence of an event which had been humanly planned, it is almost fair to say, with the express purpose of avoiding such a result. The World Missionary Conference held at Edinburgh in 1910 was the first of the great ecumenical gatherings in modern times, and is generally regarded as the beginning of this movement. When the meeting was being arranged, the church mission boards invited to send delegations were assured that there would be no discussion of doctrinal questions and that the subject of Church unity was not on the agenda. Yet out of this conference—out of an aroused awareness of the need for a sustained grappling with the issues which had been raised—and out of the consciousness of the reality of a common life in the Christian community and the service of the Evangel which had been vividly lived for a little while—came the Continuation Committee, which in turn led to the establishment of the International Missionary Council, the first of the great international interdenominational organizations. As Tomkins puts it:

> . . . it was theologically inevitable that to take seriously the Church as *Apostolic* led to the discovery of the call to the Church to be *One*. . . . to be serious about Christian witness meant by spiritual necessity to become serious about Christian unity: the World Conference on Christian Missions implied inevitably the World Conference on Faith and Order.[7]

Thus the Ecumenical Movement has in many respects taken form as an uncalculated result of other concerns of the Church. It has been filled with these surprises. Conversely, it has now begun to return to the Church an unexpected increment in areas of Christian faith and life which at first glance seem to have little direct relationship to the specific interests of co-operation and unity. Some of these extra dividends of ecumenicity are of the highest importance for the work of the preacher.

There is a further consideration that will perhaps indicate something of the sense of urgency behind the attempt to relate the Ecumenical Movement to the task of the preacher. Though many of the most significant results of the movement have been unexpected, and though all of them, being gifts of grace, are undeserved, there comes a time when they must be appropriated or they will be lost—or at least so impaired in their vitality that much of their significance and power will be withdrawn from us for a time.

The world-wide Christian community, together with the great range of corporate interests and activities that belong to it, has come into existence largely without the express design of the churches. But it will not be a vital and increasingly cohesive fellowship except as the churches own it openly and gladly, participate in its life consciously and responsibly, make use of its gifts, and continually ask to what further responses it is summoning them. This is of course a part of the significance of the constituting of the World Council. By acting to establish it, and by officially relating themselves to it, the churches have now explicitly acknowledged and claimed participation in the

Ecumenical Movement. To be sure, what this participation actually involves has different meanings for different communions. But for all of them, entrance into the World Council is in a sense an act of appropriating gifts they did not originally set out to possess—and, we may believe, of preparing to appropriate yet other gifts that have not been contemplated by the architects of the Council's affairs. As Visser 't Hooft said, prior to Amsterdam:

[The World Council] dare not minimize the very real disunity within its membership; on the other hand it may not refuse the gift of unity which the Lord has actually given and gives to the churches, when He enables them to speak and act together. . . . The World Council does not claim any authority for itself. But it must realize that it may, *Deo volente*, suddenly take on the formidable authority of an organ of the Holy Spirit. Its whole life must be a constant counting with that possibility and a constant watching for that intervention from above.[8]

As the increasing riches of the Ecumenical Movement—of which the churches more often than not have been surprised recipients rather than conscious designers—need to be acknowledged and claimed by the churches, so there are special gifts of this movement to ministers of the Word. And these now require to be explicitly recognized and accepted if they are to be firmly held and fully possessed.

In the local parish we ministers face in the most concrete way what may be called the "denominational dilemma"—the dilemma of the denominational ministry. The issue is not whether we shall be fighting denominationalists; among scholastically well-trained ministers of irenic spirit there is not in these days a great deal of "denominational preaching"; certainly not much of the quarrelsome type that stresses the rectitude of the preacher's denomination on all major points of doctrine and practice, as contrasted with the gross error of other communions. Denominationalism appears among us in less obtrusive and more comely dress. But appear it does—and given the present estate of Protestantism, it appears necessarily and rightly. When the choice is between unattached, strictly parochial, and therefore evangelically irresponsible Christianity (if that could be called "Christianity") on the one hand, and denominationalism on the other, then denominationalism is the lesser of two evils.

Here then is our plight. The Gospel of which the minister is a servant includes the fact and claim of the Church. If his message is to have evangelical point—if the claim of the Church on the hearer of the message is to evoke a response of acceptance and commitment —this response must be concrete and particular. The commitment is to a particular church—an actual congregation of the people of Christ. And in Protestantism today, commitment to a particular congregation is commitment to a congregation of a particular denomination. (In making this statement one does not except the allegedly undenominational "community churches"—which compound the ambiguity by being members of a denomination without admitting it—sometimes, one fears, without even knowing it.)

In stating the denominational dilemma one may of course invite serious misunderstanding, and appear to blunt the particularity of Christian commitment. "Why," one may ask, "if allegiance is properly given to a particular congregation may it not also be given to a particular denomination?" Nor is there the inference that these confessional loyalties—however vague the reason for them may be to our increasingly migrant Protestant community in America—are not still expressive of deep convictions and do not testify to profound realities of the Christian faith and life. The difficulty is that in the case of the denomination the particular is also partial, and the testimony to truth is to a truth that is truncated and maimed. Loyalty to the local congregation is loyalty to a body which, at least in principle, is capable of being the Church of Jesus Christ in that place. That statement is not doctrinaire Congregationalism, it is acceptable in any communion—that, under proper authorization, the congregation can manifest the fullness of the Church's life in its local dimensions. But loyalty to the denomination—and I think we are all coming to see this fact so clearly that it may be said almost categorically—is not loyalty to the wholeness of Christian truth and to membership in the fullness of the Body of Christ. The denomination is something which exists side by side with other denominations, because there is in the Christian community a withholding of full obedience to the One Lord of the Church; and the withholding is there after all allowances for disagreement due to imperfect knowledge have been made. Moreover, it exists because there is, as a consequence of withholding full obedience to Him, a withholding of fullness of fellowship one with another. The congregation is there because it is a necessary form of the Church's life, but the denomination is there, side by side with other denominations, because of a failure in the Church's obedience. A recognition of the good in denominations, and even of their necessity in an interim position, must not be allowed to deceive us concerning the failure.

Any minister who has taken his evangelistic task seriously—a task that includes the offering of the Gospel in and through the Church—and who has been concerned not merely for the initial act of Christian commitment but also for the dimensions and maturing of Christian commitment, has found himself in this denominational dilemma. This dilemma is equally apparent for the evangelistic task in its missionary aspect. Excepting only the coldness of heart in multitudes of nominal church members, there is nothing that so disastrously affects the planning and discharge of the Church's missionary vocation as does the Church's disunity.

Our present consideration is not primarily the question of Church union, especially of an organizational sort. The denominational dilemma serves mainly to point out that the ecumenical issue is practical and immediate from the standpoint of the parish minister. For the specific work of the *preaching* ministry the major significance of ecumenical developments is in the deeper movements of reformation and renewal of which the Ecumenical Movement itself is both a manifestation and, humanly speaking, an agent.

Something is *happening* in the life of the Church in our time. It appears to be a reformation as momentous as any of the reformations that have occurred in the past. Something is happening; and for the preacher of the Gospel it is important that he should try to know what is really happening behind the organized activity and underneath the conferences and discussions.

It will, perhaps, be useful to note four major points of correspondence, or convergence, of the interests which are paramount in the Ecumenical Movement and those concerns which are of central importance for the preaching ministry.

First, we do well to remember that the Ecumenical Movement has not grown out of the fondness of theologians and other scholars for conducting fireside chats on fine points of theory and doctrine. It has not taken form in the shelter of libraries and studies, though the scholars have played an indispensable role in it. The Ecumenical Movement has been forged in the fires of the Church's encounter with the crises and judgments of our time.

This fact has sometimes been made the ground of accusation. The charge is brought that the drive behind the interest in Christian unity is largely provided by what are called considerations of expediency. Ecumenicity, it is alleged, is more eager for the Church's success than for faithfulness to Christian truth. The Church, in this view, finding itself hard pressed by hostile agencies, attempts to meet these threats not with a purer witness to the Gospel but by adopting the stratagems of the world: organizing itself into larger combat units, consolidating its forces, centralizing its command. The first proposition in this argument—namely, that any response by the Church to outward crisis is necessarily suspect—should scarcely require a reply. It is of a piece with the contention that because the turbulent events of our generation have been accompanied by a deepening of theological interest, therefore this interest can be airily dismissed as a form of hysteria or combat fatigue. If there are any who still find themselves wooed by this argument, they will do well to reflect on the consequences of following it to its logical end. Remove from the Hebrew-Christian record—from the Scriptures, from the classical confessions of faith, from the testimonies of saints and seers—those portions that were produced in the times of acute social and cultural disturbance, and how much will be left? It is in just such times that the ears of men have been made receptive to hear the Word of God.

Further, it seems patent that Christian truth and the "success" of the Christian Church are not to be set in simple antithesis. Christian truth is not a series of abstract logical and theological propositions. It includes the truth that Christians are members of a body, the Church, and that this body is under orders and has a mission. Loyalty to Christian truth becomes merely academic, becomes simply the holding of correct ideas, if there is no dedication to the furtherance of this mission. To be indifferent to the estate of the Church in relation to God's purpose for it is to be recreant, from a Christian point of view, to the truth itself.

The Ecumenical Movement, then, has arisen out of a profoundly serious preoccupation with the meaning of Christian truth-in-life, truth-in-action, truth-in-community, and with the proclamation of this truth in our particular moment of history. This assuredly must also be the preoccupation of the preacher. What is the Ecumenical Movement giving us to say to the Church's situation today?

A second consideration closely akin to this is the fact that the Ecumenical Movement has developed not only in the presence of historic crisis and judgment but also in the context of *mission*. It is now a commonplace that the strongest demand and the boldest action for the union of Christians have appeared on the so-called "mission field." At the Edinburgh Conference in 1937, Bishop Azariah of India spoke memorable words to that assembly:

God in His merciful providence has used the older churches of the West to preach the gospel and found churches all over the world. Speaking as a son of one of the younger churches to our fathers in Christ in the older churches, I wish to say, we thank you for this ministry, and thank God for you. Your children by millions in every quarter of the globe have risen up and call you blessed. But we wonder if you have sufficiently contemplated the grievous sin of perpetuating your divisions and your denominational bitterness in all these your daughter churches throughout the world. We pray that those who have risen up from the younger churches and labor for union may not be considered ill-advised and hasty, lacking in theological perception and historical perspective. We want you to take us seriously when we say that the problem of union is one of life and death with us. Do not—we plead with you— do not give your aid to keep us separate, but lead us to union—so that you and we may go forward together and fulfill the prayer of our Lord.[9]

It would be interesting to know whether those words were recalled at Lambeth when Anglican relations with the Church of South India were being considered.

With the passing of the years since Edinburgh it has become more and more difficult to maintain the illusion that this appeal by an Indian bishop was conditioned by circumstances peculiar to the foreign mission field. With the progressive dechristianizing of our own society, and indeed of the whole of Western culture, we have been forced to see that the Church's mission is much the same everywhere in the world. We have seen that a church without mission is not the Church of Christ. The churches of the West, after a period of somnolence following the great epoch of expansion, are painfully recovering the truth—and in terms directly pertinent to a new situation—that "mission is the task of the Church," that, as Brunner puts it, "the Church exists by mission just as fire exists by burning." The Ecumenical Movement has advanced *pari passu* with this realization. It has come into being as we have been newly aware of both the difficulty and the desperate urgency of this mission, and have seen with fresh clarity the massiveness and power of the forces arrayed against it.

These are facts that are no less in the foreground of the preacher's consciousness than in the minds of ecumenical leaders, if he knows his field and his task. The most serious coming to grips with the problem of evangelism in our time—"the evangelization of modern man in mass society" (to use the World Council formulation)—is being undertaken under the auspices of the Study Department of the World Council. How does the Ecumenical Movement focus and empower the drive of *mission*, which must be regnant in all true preaching of the Gospel?

Third, as a part of the Ecumenical Reformation, theological work and biblical study are being carried on with a range and penetration not matched since the sixteenth century. No one would contend that these labors are proceeding exclusively or even mainly under the formal auspices of the Ecumenical Movement. But in the ecumenical setting, of which all first-rate scholarship must be continuously aware, and through the development of methods of discussion and criticism that the Ecumenical Movement has notably stimulated and sharpened, this work has acquired a distinctive vigor and pointedness for the interests of the preacher. For in this setting the scholarly enterprise has been kept vividly conscious of its responsibility to the Church and its bearing on the Church's proclamation.

This theological and biblical work has a qualitative scope, a fullness, which would be impossible outside the ecumenical context; and even those of us who are far from being able to grasp all that is being said in the discussion cannot miss this quality. Oliver Tomkins, after listing some of the most distinguished members of this company of workers—Maritain, Berdyaev, Niebuhr, Temple, Brunner, Eliot, Demant, Barth—remarks that anyone who can define what these thinkers have in common may be in a position to define the contents of the ecumenical mind. It is certainly not similarity of viewpoint and conclusion. It is, he believes, "a *wholeness* of mind which comes from praying, reading, and thinking in wider company." It is not necessary to be able to follow these leaders in every subtlety of their thought if we are to have the "ecumenical mind"; but it is necessary, Tomkins insists, "to be interested in the things they are interested in." [10]

One would add that the work of thinking in wider company has a peculiar urgency for us in America. One reason for the slowness of the American churches in developing fluent communication concerning the central issues of their common life stems from the fact that during a long period of theological triviality many of the persons most influential in American Protestantism were simply not interested in the considerations that have characteristically occupied responsible Christian thinkers in all generations.

There is abundant evidence that new gifts of intellectual grasp and spiritual insight are given to those who have taken up difficult and concrete tasks in relation to the Church's struggle for unity. This is true not only of the study commissions that labor under the auspices of the World Council of Churches and the many groups that have worked in preparation for the various ecumenical gatherings, but of those who have struggled to solve specific problems of church union or to deal with issues raised in more limited interdenominational conversations. I cannot think of a recent book in which the fundamentals of the Christian faith have been more trenchantly set forth than one by a missionary bishop (a Scottish Presbyterian bishop, by the way!) of the newly united Church of South India, a book called *The Reunion of the Church*, by Lesslie Newbigin.[11] All through it is evidence of a theological grip that has been strengthened by seizing the concrete problems of the South India union.

The results of discussions now going on in Britain among Anglo-

Catholics, Anglican Evangelicals, and a group from the Free Churches make exciting theological reading. A small book from the Free Church representatives, called *The Catholicity of Protestantism*,[12] is an extraordinarily vigorous and irenic statement of Protestant views of fundamental doctrinal issues.

Nor is this interest in matters that characteristically concern responsible Christians limited to those who are, so to speak, full-time professional theologians. Some of the statements coming from the Church of South India—particularly those in reply to questions raised by Lambeth and the Anglican Communion—are the works of groups that include pastors and laymen. One is impressed by the theological maturity of these statements, by the courteous but firm confidence that is possible only when a group has carefully worked its way through to a position. One is impressed also by their conviction that through the long process of questioning, discussing, becoming discouraged, waiting, and then being shown the way, they have been given a wonderful gift of God's mercy, which they hold humbly but exultantly in their keeping for others who will claim it. The Ecumenical Movement is thus stimulating a vigorous and responsible kind of Christian thinking which is surely one of the signs of new reformation.

Finally, in the Ecumenical Movement the Church is engaged in asking in a new and urgent way the central questions about itself and the meaning of its life. What is the Church? How is it given existence, and why in all its misery and infidelity does it continue of God's mercy to exist? What is it appointed to be and to do? In the Ecumenical Movement the Church is asking these questions not only seriously but in the supreme seriousness of repentance.

Several years ago Reinhold Niebuhr published an article entitled "The Reunion of the Church through the Renewal of the Churches," with much of which many of us are no doubt in warm agreement. "The unity of the churches," said Niebuhr, "does not as such renew the Church." He then pointed out that much of the Church's penitence for its disunity seems to stop with contrition for the sins of sectarian pride and stubbornness that keep us apart and prevent the manifestation of the Church's glory and power, and that a deeper penitence is required wherein we know that the whole life of the

Church—including its glory and power—has at all times to be brought under God's judgment. Said Niebuhr:

> We do not gain the authority to speak to the nations by achieving the prestige of organizational unity. The authority to speak to the nations is in a Gospel which discloses a majesty and a mercy beyond all historic majesties and all human justice. When that Gospel is preached with power it will heal both the nations and the church. But it will first wound the pride and self-esteem of the churches as much as the vainglory of the nations.[13]

All this is undeniably true; yet a close rereading of Niebuhr's statement makes one wonder whether he has given full weight to the question of how much the Church's struggle to overcome its disunity is in fact a mode of the Church's repentance. Has he taken account of the degree to which a failure to engage in this struggle and a willingness to remain in disunity provide a special temptation to self-esteem and pride? And there is also the question whether this disunity does not result in the Church's giving a testimony of vainglory which multitudes of Christians do not really feel in their hearts.

We have to recognize a reciprocal relationship here. If denominations are in part the creations of pride of opinion and custom, they must also be recognized as incentives to pride and perpetuators of pride. The denomination, in its nature, exerts a subtle but continuous pressure on its members to justify its existence. They have to justify it not by claims of catholicity, but, because there are other denominations, by claims of distinctiveness. And justification on grounds of alleged distinctiveness almost inevitably becomes justification on grounds of alleged superiority. Pretensions to denominational superiority, however, will nearly always appear to the surrounding community and the world as being greater than are actually made—and much greater than are actually felt—by those who are under necessity of explaining, justifying, and serving the separate existence of the denomination. Thus denominationalism impedes unnecessarily the witness of the Church to its message of contrition and repentance. It proclaims to the world a degree of loyalty to the traditions of men which great numbers of Christians do not really cherish.

The struggle for unity may be a profound form of the Church's repentance. Is it not learning in this ecumenical encounter to come under that judgment that begins at the house of God, and to ask "What are the fruits meet for repentance that must now be brought forth from the Church itself?" It is having to ask that question in the most searching way, not only concerning its most obvious sins but concerning its goodness. The things that are being brought under judgment are good and precious things—the riches of our traditions, valuable testimonies to neglected truths some portion of which every communion has helped to preserve or restore to the Church, the memories of saints and servants nurtured in all our separate households. The Church is having to learn the strange truth that it is called to repent of things whereby it has been blessed and has been a means of blessing.

And there is the question (perhaps the most searching of all) that is put to us by our ecumenical failures. Why has so little change been wrought, with all this drive of conviction that a new order in the Church ought to be brought about? Here is a great mystery of the Church: that it exists solely, in so far as it truly exists as the Church, by dependence on its living Head, and yet in its inmost life, its own fellowship and order can be persistently disobedient to Him. In the mystery of our ecumenical failure the Church sees, and the preacher sees—perhaps more clearly than in any other context—the standpoint from which the Church's proclamation is to be made. Every word of judgment and promise the Church speaks to the world must be uttered out of the acknowledgment of its own need of forgiveness. And this shattering acknowledgment is possible from the depths of a faith that knows this other and supreme mystery: that we are forgiven.

This questioning in depth concerning the nature and meaning of the Church's own life, in which the Ecumenical Movement is engaged, is a matter of the most central relevance for us as preachers of the Word in the Church.

What is the resource that the Ecumenical Movement mediates to the preacher? It is not merely giving the setting of his message new dimension and amplitude. Rather it is the resource that comes from the fact that the whole Church, through being driven into the depths where it confronts with an absolute seriousness the questions pertaining to its very life, has found deeper meaning in the renewing Gospel. All this is present for the preacher to claim for his message.

What is the command? It is that the wholeness of the Church's life as we are now being given to know it, the fullness of its catholic faith and the concreteness of its existence as a people—the people of Christ who are being regathered and reconstituted in our time—shall be resonant in the preacher's word.

In a sixteenth century Confession of Faith of the churches of France there is a terse description of the Reformers. They are, says this Confession, "people whom God has raised up in an extraordinary manner to build anew the Church which was in ruin and desolation." Those whom God has raised up in our day to build anew the Church are many, and they work most often in quiet and unspectacular ways. Speaking to the Church from within the Church concerning its ruin and desolation may not be as simply convincing as in some generations, for in many respects the Church seems to be strong and full of health. But in this new encounter with the Gospel, for which the Ecumenical Movement is an important means, many have known the true desolation of the Church, namely, the separation of Christians from their Lord, and thus from one another. Many have also known the grievous ruin of the Church, which is that in its separation it shares and consents in the ruin of the world.

Yet in precisely this humiliation—and how else does renewal from God ever come?—God is raising up many for the building anew, the remaking, the reformation of His Church.

The greatest contribution that the Church can make to the renewal of society is for it to be renewed in its own life in faith and obedience to its Lord. Such inner renewal includes a clearer grasp of the meaning of the Gospel for the whole life of man.

From the FIRST ASSEMBLY OF THE WORLD COUNCIL OF CHURCHES [1]

We must all listen together in the midst of our disunity to our one Lord speaking to us through Holy Scripture. This is a hard thing to do. We still struggle to comprehend the meaning and authority of Holy Scripture. Yet whenever we are prepared to undertake together the study of the Word of God and are resolved to be obedient to what we are told, we are on the way toward realizing the oneness of the Church in Christ in the actual state of our dividedness on earth.

From the SECOND ASSEMBLY OF THE WORLD COUNCIL OF CHURCHES [2]

The Bible is to be understood in the fellowship of the whole Church, but the traditions of the Church are to be judged in the light of the Bible. . . . The Church is liable to error and has erred. When she treats her own traditions as finally normative, she delivers herself over in a kind of bondage which Christ never imposed to a law which is not the law of God. She is to live always in penitent and alert obedience to her living Lord, and she has the revelation of His nature and the record of His mighty acts done for her redemption in those Scriptures which she has treasured from the days of those who were witnesses of them. These, therefore, are her supreme and decisive standard of faith, and to these she must ever turn, knowing that as she exposes herself afresh to the Gospel of which the Scriptures are the record, she will receive afresh the guiding of the Holy Spirit as to the present will of her Lord.

LESSLIE NEWBIGIN [3]

CHAPTER II

The Renewing Word

WHAT are the sources and agencies of the Church's renewal, which, as Amsterdam reminded us, must precede any effective action by the Church for the renewal of society? One cannot follow the movements of ecumenical thought without knowing that it has focused on a certainty that a chief means to this inner renewal of the Church is a more alert attentiveness to the message of the Bible. A condition of renewal of faith and obedience to the Church's Lord is that we shall hear more clearly the Word of the Lord.

The New Reformation, like the earlier one, is to be characterized by saying that it looks for "reformation according to the Word of God." It is marked, as was the sixteenth century renewal, by an eager, expectant, and profoundly serious turning to the Bible. As the earlier reformers rediscovered the inherent power of the scriptures, the Ecumenical Reformation is also a corporate rediscovering of the wholly unique power of the Bible to speak to man in the dimension of his darkest misery, his most abysmal need, his most instant hope. It is also an acknowledgment that this power has been diverted and very often negated by the traditions of men.

One may fairly say that the Ecumenical Movement in all its conversations and studies has been persistently and intensely preoccupied with two central subjects: first, the nature of the Church; and second, the character and meaning of the Word of God. It has also recognized that these concerns are indivisible; that the subjects are so intimately interrelated that the one cannot be dealt with apart from the other, and that if they are separated in discussion it is only for pur-

poses of orderly treatment. The indissoluble character of this relationship is seen when we consider, from the one side, that the
Church is constituted by the Word of God, of which the Bible is
the witness, and that it owes its existence moment by moment to that
living Word, and from the other side that it is in the Church and
only in the Church that the Word of God in the Bible is known and
interpreted. To speak of the Church is to speak of that community
which is given life and renewal by the Word to which constant
witness is made in the Bible. To speak of the Bible is to speak of
that Book which the Church confesses to be Scripture. Neither
Church nor Bible is truly viewed until they are both seen together.

Some temporary separation is necessary, however, for orderly
speech, and in this chapter we shall be concerned with the influence
of the Ecumenical Movement in the task of reformation according
to the Word of God, at the point of its inevitable dependence on a
new hearing of the Word in the Bible. We shall try to see something
of what the Ecumenical Movement has done to enrich and clarify
our understanding of this Word, the Word that is witnessed to in
the Scriptures and understood by the illumination of the Holy Spirit
in the Church.

For one who has some realization that there is a difference between a *student* of the Bible (which every Christian minister and
indeed every Christian ought to be) and a biblical *scholar* (which
few of us are either called or able to be), a good deal of audacity is
required to approach even the periphery of this theme.

If the nonscholarly commentator on this subject has grave dis-
abilities, he may perhaps claim one small advantage. It is the advantage of the plainsman who stood on the rim of the Grand Canyon
and remarked that he was experiencing a decided enlargement of his
conception of a ditch. Many of the issues and conclusions dealt with
in ecumenical conversation are doubtless commonplace enough to
the biblical scholar, but they come to the ordinary inquirer with exciting freshness and sense of discovery. In some of the ecumenical
documents is gathered and summarized the most vigorous contemporary scholarship of the Church. To those who are professionally
engaged in this work and are continuously in touch with the studies
and conclusions of many colaborers in the field, the changes in view-

point that have occurred during let us say the past twenty-five years may seem unspectacular. For them these changes have been cumulative and gradual. But for those of us who have been busy with other matters, who have not maintained this continuous and close-range view of the specialist, there is a kind of dramatic magnitude both in the changes of viewpoint of biblical scholars and in the approach to a consensus among them. Probably there is no better vantage point from which to see these developments than the one provided by the records of ecumenical conversations.

We may make bold to say that as a consequence of the work of ecumenical biblical scholarship (and of course all first-rate scholarship is now ecumenical), and as a consequence of reflection on and discussion of this work in an ecumenical setting, the Bible in its wholeness has been given back to the preacher. It has been repossessed and made available in a more direct and relevant way than at any time since the Reformation as a Book that has been given us for the purpose—perhaps for the sole purpose—of being preached. This return of the Book to the preacher has occurred after a long period during which biblical study was marked by toil among stretches of evangelical aridity. It may have been a necessary period; certainly the men who are now working in more fruitful ground are immeasurably indebted to those who cleared the land and sharpened the indispensable tools for their present labors. But almost in our own time— within the time when the ecumenical enterprise has been taking shape—the Bible has become known as a Book of Proclamation, the bearer of a message, the communicator of something to be told. So it has been restored to the hands of the preacher in a way that is both constraining and liberating.

Let us consider what is involved in this restoration.

When we say, as frequently has been said, that in the churches touched by ecumenical interest there has occurred a notable "back to the Bible" movement, we are perhaps lacking careful discrimination, for it must be remembered that many of these churches have never turned away from the Bible. We must recall, too, that other churches, which seemed for a while to subordinate the Bible to something called "the Christian attitude" or even to "the spirit of modern thought," or to a moral perfectionism derived from the

Sermon on the Mount in disregard of much of the rest of the Bible,
never disavowed their confession that the Bible provides the supreme
standard of Christian faith and life. What seems actually to have
occurred is not so much that a forgotten Bible has been remembered
as that the Bible has become again in a living and intensely vivid
way a common possession—or, more accurately, has become again
the supreme witness to that by which we are all possessed. When it
is asked, "What do Christians have in common?" one answer
assuredly is, "The Bible." And this answer is much more than formal
or honorific; it is an answer at once profoundly personal and corporate. To be a Christian is to stand in a certain relationship to that
which comes to us through the Bible. What God has done for us in
Christ is not known apart from this Book. To be a Christian is to
confess by faith that this Bible, speaking to us of what God has done,
is Holy Scripture, that it has power to make us hear His Word.
Further, this Bible is not only the Book of the Christian person, it
is the Book of a people—of this people: the Christian community—
which it has called and continually calls into being as the people of
Christ. And the service of the preacher is to hear this call, which cannot be heard apart from the Bible, and to make it vocal and living
and immediate in the life of the Church.

The focusing of biblical inquiry on preaching has been sharpened
in ecumenical discourse. This has come about very naturally because
the Ecumenical Movement, being of and for the Church, has directed
biblical study to questions of the meaning of the Bible for the
Church—and for the Church's proclamation. Not that the Christian
biblical scholar is likely to be unaware that his critical and expository
work is always in the service of the Church; but that in the context
of the Ecumenical Movement it has been impossible to forget this
fact or to subordinate it even for a moment. The churchly character
of biblical study—its relevance to the message and mission of the
Church—is the sole raison d'être for such study carried on ecumenically. Moreover, in the ecumenical context biblical study is
pursued by the participants with a maximum sense of responsibility.
Here the attention of the Church is fixed on one of the issues most
clearly determinative for its unity. Though not all communions may
assent to the assertion that continuity in the succession of the

Apostles' message is the primary meaning of apostolic succession, all
would be agreed that it is one of the essential meanings. Therefore
in trying to understand the nature of this catholicity and the grounds
of catholic unity we have to ask what the message of the Apostles
actually was. An inseparable part of the question, "How far are we
agreed concerning the message of the Church?" is the prior question,
"To what extent do we find the same meaning in the Bible?"

Aware of the magnitude of the issues dependent on their work,
those who engage in this task find themselves involved in a fresh encounter with the Bible as it meets them in the ecumenical environment. This is evident both from the testimony of persons who have
participated in the study and from the quality of the published material that is beginning to come out of these conversations. The
Word of the Bible is being heard in a new way. In an atmosphere
of Christian candor, partial views, conditioned by time and place and
church tradition, are exposed for correction. Members find themselves listening, every one to the others and all together listening
anew to the Bible itself. Says a statement from one of these groups:

. . . In applying the Biblical message to our day interpreters diverge
because of differing doctrinal and ecclesiastical traditions, differing
ethical, political, and cultural outlooks, differing geographical and socio-
logical situations, differing temperaments and gifts. It is, however, an
actual experience within the Ecumenical Movement, that when we meet
together, with presuppositions of which we may be largely unconscious,
and bring these presuppositions to the judgment of Scripture some of
the very difficulties are removed which prevent the Gospel from being
heard. Thus the Bible itself leads us back to the living Word of God.[4]

Perhaps the most spectacular manifestation of the creative nature
of this ecumenical encounter occurred at the Bossey study conference
sponsored by the World Council in 1947. There the two leading
Continental theologians, Nygren and Barth, stood up one after the
other to declare that "so far as they were concerned the historic conflict between Lutheran and Calvinist theology was at an end
—resolved through a common understanding of the Bible's main
message to our times." [5]

The significance for the preacher of this ecumenical repossession of the Bible derives not only from the fruitfulness of the interpretive work it is stimulating but also from the present situation of the preacher himself. This quickened attentiveness to the Bible has appeared at a time when there is a vast uneasiness among us preachers over the inadequacy of a message not sufficiently grounded in the scriptural revelation. It is not necessary for us to be "Barthians" in order to understand a little of the radical self-questioning—the "embarrassment," as he calls it—that drove Karl Barth to undertake his great critical work.

We do not need to be Barthians to recognize how penetrating is Barth's description of the preacher's embarrassment. Parenthetically, there are encouraging signs that point to a new reluctance on the part of ministers today about joining the parade of those who not long ago became crusading anti-Barthians without having read a page of anything Barth had written. It is to be hoped that some of us may even refrain from quoting bright anti-Barthian aphorisms coined by clever phrasemakers who also have not read Barth. No other thinker of our time has suffered as much from this compounding of critical ignorance; the sweeping judgment of somebody who has no acquaintance with his work, based on the sweeping judgment of somebody else who likewise has no acquaintance with his work, and so on through a vast chain reaction of Barthian illiteracy. While Barth is rugged enough to survive this kind of misrepresentation, it does not encourage attention to the very important things he has to say. It is especially a pity when we preachers are discouraged from listening to him, when we are afraid that if we are caught with Volume One of the *Dogmatics* on our shelves we will be haled before a church security board and judged subversive Barthians. It is a pity, because Barth is the preacher's theologian *par excellence*. "The normal and central fact with which *Dogmatics* has to do," he says, "is, very simply, the church's Sunday sermon of yesterday and tomorrow." Few experiences are likely to come to us as preachers which can be at once so shattering and so cleansing as that of allowing the Swiss theologian to conduct us, step by step, to the place where we really know for ourselves the acuteness of the preacher's "embarrassment."

Barth has not written many passages of autobiography, and would doubtless regard the few excursions of this sort as trivia. But at least

one personal testimony is highly illuminating, and there might be
much less misunderstanding of his position and purpose if this confession could be remembered when we read his more formal theological writings. It reminds us that his whole work, one may almost
say, has been a mighty grappling with the question, "What is it to
preach, and why do we preach at all?" In an address to a conference
of ministers, Barth said:

For twelve years I was a minister, as all of you are. I had my theology.
It was not really mine, to be sure, but that of my unforgotten teacher,
Wilhelm Hermann. . . . Once in the ministry, I found myself growing
away from these theological habits of thought and being forced back at
every point more and more upon the specific minister's problem, the
sermon. I sought to find my way between the problem of human life on
the one hand and the content of the Bible on the other. As a minister
I wanted to speak to the people in the infinite contradiction of their life,
but to speak the no less infinite message of the Bible, which was as much
of a riddle as life. Often enough these two magnitudes, life and the
Bible, have risen before me (and still rise!) like Scylla and Charybdis: if
these are the whence and whither of Christian preaching, who shall, who
can, be a minister and preach? . . . [So] it came about that this familiar
situation of the minister on Saturday at his desk and on Sunday in his
pulpit crystallized in my case into a marginal note to all theology, which
finally assumed the voluminous form of a complete commentary on the
Epistle to the Romans. . . .

It is not as if I had found any way out of this critical situation. Exactly not that. But this critical situation itself became to me an explana-
tion of the character of all theology. What else can theology be but the
truest possible expression of this quest and questioning on the part of
the minister, the description of this embarrassment into which a man
falls when he ventures upon this task and out of which he cannot
find his way—a cry for rescue arising from great need and great hope?
What better can theology do to fulfill its cultural task—and it has such
—and its pedagogical task . . . what better can it do as it sets forth its
traditional, historical, systematic, and practical material than to be con-
stantly aware that in its essential and innermost idea it must be the
description of an embarrassment? . . .

Would it not pay, I asked myself further, to satisfy one's self how
much light might be shed upon theology from this viewpoint? Would it
not be for theology's own good if it attempted, as I have said, to be

nothing more than this knowledge of the quest and questioning of the Christian preacher, full of need and full of promise? . . . Oppressed by the question . . . I finally went to work upon the Epistle to the Romans, which first was to be only an essay to help me to know my own mind. Naturally and evidently there are many subjects mentioned in the book—New Testament theology, dogmatics, ethics, and philosophy— but you will best understand it when you hear through it all, the minister's question: What is preaching?—not How *does* one do it? but How can one do it? [6]

It is probably fair to say that the ecumenical studies and conversations dealing with the Bible have been marked by a continuous engrossment with this radical questioning. The question is the preacher's question, the question of Church proclamation. How does one find the way "between the problem of human life on the one hand and the content of the Bible on the other," between the world of modern thought and that "strange new world within the Bible," of which Barth spoke, whose outlook is so different and alien? This constant and resolute relating of Bible study to the message of the Church is one of the major concerns of ecumenical investigation.

One further result of contemporary biblical work carried on in the ecumenical setting is the restoration of the unity of scriptural study with the other disciplines which are to be put at the service of Christian proclamation—for example: historical, systematic, and practical theology. For a time the vigor of these disciplines was threatened by the same notions of autonomy which have had such a stultifying effect in general education and modern culture. It was imagined by some biblical scholars that by a sufficiently acute examination of the text, an examination guided by recognized historical and linguistic criteria, one could find out what the Bible really says. At the same time, theologians tended to set up their own norms without the regulation of Scripture, and these norms became increasingly speculative and rationalistic. Thus Harnack, having found portions of the Bible incongruous with his independent theological views, proposed the elimination of the Old Testament from the canon of Christian Scriptures. In our time there has been a notable change of direction, which is now toward restoration of the interdependence and unity of these disciplines.

From the one side, the biblical student continually reminds the theologian of the scriptural vehicle of Christian revelation—that it is just this Book, with its account of concrete events in which God has acted for man's redemption that is the *locus* of His Word; that when we are able to hear that Word in other places it is only because we have first been addressed by it through the Bible. The biblical scholar, therefore, continually reminds the theologian of the scriptural foundation of all his work.

From the other side, the theologian presses home to the biblical scholar the fact that historical study and literary investigation have no significance for Christian proclamation when they are carried on outside the context of Christian theology. The Bible has to be interpreted, and it has to be interpreted from the viewpoint of a radical conviction that this Word speaks of *God*, that is, from the viewpoint of a theology.

Then the biblical student re-enters the conversation, to recall to the theologian that while interpretation is necessary it is not an untrammelled exercise of reason and spiritual imagination; that the Bible itself sets limits to the freedom of the interpreter. There are objective criteria to be respected. These words, through which God has spoken and may speak again today, are also human words, spoken at a particular time and place and in particular circumstances. They were spoken in a particular language. They were spoken by and to particular persons. These particularities cannot be disregarded in deciding what the Bible says; and a message that seems at the moment to be theologically consistent, or culturally acceptable, or ecclesiastically edifying, or even evangelically persuasive, may not be the message of the Bible. There are ministers who make the Bible evangelically effective, on their own terms, in curious ways. They use biblical quotations to assure people that they are wonderfully fine folks and that they can have peace of mind and cure their worries and find success if they will only think well enough of themselves and learn the art of confident living. There are people who find this "message" very welcome and persuasive, and who respond by coming back for more. But it is not the message of the Bible concerning our human situation. There are objective norms, historical and textual,

that control our interpretation of what the Bible says, and it is the
business of the biblical scholar to see that these are kept in mind.

But once again the theologian speaks. And now he reminds the
biblical scholar that the God to whom the Bible bears witness is the
living God, and His Word is a living and contemporaneous Word.
Therefore the message of the Bible is not discerned when we know
as precisely and fully as possible what God once *said* to the men of
olden time but when we subject ourselves to its power to make us
hear what God *says* to us today.

The fact that this exchange of thought has been set in dialogue
form may seem to suggest that there is a controversy between the
biblical scholar and the theologian, and that each discipline is made
aware of its dependence on the other only under pressure of persistent reminder. But the actual situation is that the acknowledgment
of this interdependence and unity is now axiomatic. Theology has
become increasingly biblical, and biblical study has become steadily
more aware that it must be theological.

It would be claiming too much to say that the Ecumenical Movement has been solely responsible for this unitive tendency among the
various disciplines that have bearing on the Church's proclamation.
But it has certainly exerted a very great influence. As representatives
of the various communions have conversed with one another about
the message and mission of the Church, they have had to articulate
their view with a wholeness and adequacy that may not be necessary
when the subject is more technical. In ecumenical discourse these
disciplines are brought to the most vivid awareness of their mutual
dependence, because they are brought to a common service of the
Church and its testimony.

Before commenting briefly on the main emphases of biblical
interpretation and the impressive consensus that this ecumenical
enterprise of grappling with the meaning of the Bible is now offering us, it is well to make one further observation about the spirit and
quality of the investigations now being carried on. There is an
opinion in some quarters that some of the most influential scholars
in the field are proceeding in disregard, or even in rejection, of the
critical work of the past century. The casual reader skims the reports
of ecumenical studies and discussions, and notes the use of terms

that he associates with traditionalist or even "fundamentalist" views. He sees references, for example, to the witness of the Old Testament to Christ, or he observes these studies taking very seriously the eschatological outlook of the Bible, and he immediately concludes that we are faced with a resurgence of literalism.

It would be difficult to overstate the enormity of this misunderstanding. The constructive enterprise now going forward would be inconceivable without the critical work of the past century. There is not the slightest disposition in ecumenical study to return to a precritical point of view. This has been emphasized repeatedly in statements from the Study Department of the World Council, and the representatives of the churches participating in the conversations are wholly agreed on this point. In a recent publication of the Study Department the following statement appeared:

> It is very important to note that in speaking of "the Biblical doctrine of . . ." we do not mean any treatment of the Biblical material which would suggest a literalistic use of the Bible. We want to learn what light the Biblical message as a whole—Old and New Testament, centered in the message of the crucified and risen Lord Jesus Christ—throws on our problems. This calls for thoroughgoing historical, critical and theological exegesis, the methods of which have been discussed at different ecumenical conferences and should constantly be reconsidered and improved.[7]

We cannot appreciate the quality of these biblical studies until we have some conception of the tremendous critical discipline that is being brought to bear upon the task. The scholarly principles employed are no less rigorous than in the days when vast labors were spent upon the minutiae of the text, but these principles have been extended and made more comprehensive. They have particularly been extended to include the critic as well as the material with which he is working. A previously cited statement from the World Council Study Department speaks of the "unconscious presuppositions" that are brought to the interpretation of the Bible. Much of the critical work of recent times, especially in ecumenical discourse, has aimed at exposing these presuppositions of the interpreter, which are imposed on the Bible and thus get in the way of hearing what the Bible itself has to say. The possibility of a purely "objective" approach to the Bible—of the interpreter's approaching it without any presuppositions acquired from extrabiblical sources which he then proceeds to read into the Bible—is as unlikely as the *tabula rasa* theory of the mind. One of the great contributions of ecumenical study, as the World Council statement points out, arises from the fact that in these conversations the unconscious presuppositions of one person are recognized by others—who also, of course, have their own unconscious presuppositions but not the same as the first man's.

To know at least in a general way the method and purpose of this constructive ecumenical study seems to me of the utmost importance for us as preachers. It is a plain matter of the responsible discharge of our ministerial office and of fidelity to our ordination vows. We are appointed to open the Scriptures to the people of the Church. But how much of the preaching done in recent times is the opening not of the Scripture but of the preacher's own thought, giving it a spurious authority by misuse of the Scripture, and at the same time evading the drastic message of the Bible itself. Not infrequently this evasion is abetted by our knowledge of the so-called "critical approach to the Bible," the critical approach which neglects to be critical of the critic.

We are highly sophisticated about the human elements that entered into the formation and selection of the canon of Scripture; but we can be terribly naïve about the canonizing of our own opinions, and the extent to which, in practice, we select a private canon of Scripture on the basis of our own presuppositions. We recognize "folklore in the Bible," and forget the enormous folklore of modern secularism which the Bible is distorted to sanction. We reject the allegorical method of interpretation common in precritical times, and then proceed to a new and perhaps more misleading form of allegorizing, which is the imposition upon the Bible of the allegories of modern thought—the allegory of organic growth, for example, and the allegory of cause-and-effect continuity.

The direction of ecumenical study is in a very real sense toward a reapplication of the reformers' principle, *Scriptura Scripturae interpres*—"Scripture is the interpreter of Scripture." There is a new readiness to take seriously the Bible's own view of itself. Before we impose upon it our theories as to what it is—the history of an ancient nation, the record of the progressive moral and spiritual understanding of a people "with a genius for religion," the story of a supremely exemplary human life, and so on—before selecting any of these, or all of them, as adequate appraisals of what the Bible is, we may do well to consider what the Bible-in-the-Church itself professes to be: a witness to what God has done for our salvation. Ecumenical study has been asking: Can any method of criticism be sound if it leaves us in the position of judging the Bible, and fails to bring us finally to the place where the Bible judges us? Can any method of investigation be valid, however much it may illuminate historical and philological facts, if it obscures the central fact of what the Bible represents itself to be—a testimony concerning the mighty acts of God wrought for our redemption?

This survey of the method and purpose of the ecumenical study of the Bible may seem to have led us into a realm of technical problems where none but the professional scholar is competent to evaluate the quality of the work being done. Yet all of us, as ministers, are forced to an evaluation. As a result of the work of criticism and interpretation, the Bible is being given to us with new livingness and power. It is a matter of the greatest moment that we should decide to what extent we can have confidence in the underlying scholarly labor and in the scholars who are performing it: their thoroughness, their openness to teaching by one another and by the Bible itself, their sense of responsibility to the Gospel and the Church, the committed quality of their toil. And what we are really evaluating here— and what we all have some competence to appraise—is not so much a critical method as a method by which critical methods are themselves subjected to criticism. It is the ecumenical method. It is much more than the normal interscholastic and international traffic that goes on among all scholars. It is more than the interconfessional exchange and submission to mutual criticism in which Christian scholars have long engaged. It is essentially a new method of study and investigation.

What have been the results of this ecumenical study of the Bible?

They have in fact been so many and so important that any answer to that question must be given in the form of samples and intimations rather than in any comprehensive catalog of achievements.

First, there has come about a quite astonishing agreement around basic principles of biblical interpretation. In the summer of 1949 a study conference was held at Oxford, England, to deal with the problem of relating the biblical message to social and political questions. Two similar conferences had already been held, and this meeting built on the results of the earlier sessions. The group included some of the most vigorous minds in the Church. The diversities of tradition are indicated by the membership of the conference, which included an Anglican (Canon Alan Richardson), an Indian Baptist (Prof. V. E. Devadutt of Bengal), a Swedish Lutheran (Bishop Anders Nygren), an American Presbyterian (Prof. G. E. Wright of Chicago), a member of the Russian Orthodox Church (Prof. Georges Florovsky), an English Congregationalist (Prof. C. H. Dodd), an American Methodist (the late Dean Clarence T. Craig) and about a dozen others equally representative and competent.

Members of this group have said that the most illuminating periods in their week of corporate study were not the times when they were conversing about the Bible but when they actually opened the Bible to a particular passage and considered what the Bible said to them and how far they could agree as to what it said.

At the end of this period of work they were able to give common assent to a set of principles of biblical interpretation. They found, as they reported, "a measure of agreement that surprised us all." They were agreed on basic theological presuppositions that they believed necessary for biblical interpretation: that "the Bible is our common starting point, for there God's Word confronts us, a Word which humbles the hearers so that they are more ready to listen and discuss than they are to assert their own opinions"; that the central message of the Bible is the action of God for the saving of man, "that He might create in Jesus Christ a people for Himself"; that "the centre and goal of the Bible is Christ," and that this gives the Old and New Testaments a unity in which Christ "is seen both as the fulfillment and the end of the Law"; that "the starting point of the Christian interpreter lies within the redeemed community of which by faith he is a member."

In wrestling with the problem of applying biblical teaching to the Church's social and political message, the scholars were agreed that the law of love has always a binding and compelling hold on us, and in it we encounter the inescapable will of God. On the other hand, in the more specific laws provided for the detailed organisation of the social life of a people who lived under conditions different from our own, we should through reverent and serious study seek to distinguish in the light of God's revelation in Christ the permanently binding from that of purely local and temporal significance.[8]

(No precritical literalism here!) The scholars rejected the possibility of finding any simple identity of social situation between the biblical world and contemporary life. "Nevertheless," they said, "in each new situation we must allow ourselves to be guided by the Bible to a knowledge of the will of God." They agreed that "the Bible speaks primarily to the Church, but it also speaks through the Church to the world inasmuch as the whole world is claimed by the Church's Lord. The Church can best speak to the world by becoming the Church remade by the Word of God."

This consensus on the basic principles of interpretation may not seem at first glance to be of revolutionary significance. Yet when we consider the diverse character of the group and the fact that every one of the areas in which agreement was found has been in former times a scene of theological carnage, the degree of unanimity is astonishing. Some of the widest chasms that have separated families of Christians from one another are perceptibly narrowed by these agreements. An example is the statement concerning the relation of Scripture and tradition. This has special importance because of the position of Eastern Orthodoxy, which affirms that the Bible and the holy tradition of the Church have equal authority. Yet with two representatives of the Orthodox churches present, the scholars were able to say: "It is agreed that although we may differ in the manner in which tradition, reason and natural law may be used in the interpretation of Scripture, any teaching that clearly contradicts the Biblical position cannot be accepted as Christian." Does not this view, if it be acceptable to Eastern Orthodoxy, make Scripture actually normative and place it in a position superior to tradition, at least on those matters concerning which the Bible speaks at all, since tradition is not to be contradictory of Scripture? The willingness to listen together to the message of the Bible is disclosing new possibilities for the removal of some of the most obstructive barriers that have kept Christians apart.

Second, a central meaning in all this discussion (and the minister must consider how widely representative of competent scholarship this understanding has now come to be) is that the Bible is viewed as having a living unity. It is genuinely the Word, not just many words. It has a unity which was almost lost to sight during the period of biblical fragmentation, of organizing the Bible on various "levels," of separating the primitive from the more recent and then discarding the primitive on the assumption there is always an advance beyond it. We are now seeing that when the Bible is read in the community of faith, where it is known as Holy Scripture, it is in a profound sense one book. As a member of the World Council study group has written:

> . . . Every passage belongs to a larger whole. We read a passage within the context of the whole original writing. We interpret an oracle or confession of Jeremiah or a passage from Paul in the light of the entire book. But the books themselves belong to a single organic unity. They are part of a covenant literature. They are part of a continuing revelation which assumes for the Christian the character of a "story" in which the purpose of God is at work in the world. In this story we inevitably read all things in the light of the beginning and end. . . . We cannot select certain passages and eliminate others from this story. Otherwise the anthologist determines where revelation is present and where it is not.[9]

The well-nigh universal acceptance of this principle of the unity of Scripture is evident in what is in many ways the most impressive product to date of the ecumenical study of the Bible. *Biblical Authority for Today* is the work of a group of distinguished scholars, most of whom have participated in the study conferences held under the auspices of the World Council of Churches. With these scholars the principle of the unity of the Bible has now become almost axiomatic. The Scripture as a whole is "salvation history." When this is seen, the Bible is understood to have a single theme that underlies all its diversities and particularities. Its integrity is given it by the fact that it tells of one God, working through one event— the total event of Jesus Christ, for one purpose—the saving of sinful

man through the creation of a people who shall know Him as God
and make known His lordship to all mankind. The unity of the
Bible is thus not literary, nor ideological, nor developmental. It is
the living unity of a drama in which there is always one supreme
Actor, ultimately controlling all events and working through them
for the doing of one decisive deed. John Marsh, a member of the
biblical study group, characterizes this unity in a series of summary
statements. (1) "The same God is the subject of the story of both
Old and New Testaments." (2) "The same God offers in the two
Testaments the same salvation." (3) "In both Testaments the same
God offers the same salvation by the same Saviour." (4) "In both
Testaments the same God offers the same salvation by the same
Saviour through the same actions."

God, Christians believe, has acted decisively to save man in Jesus
Christ. But that one act of God was possible only through a whole series
of historical events, which centered indeed in the life and death and
resurrection of Jesus Christ, but which of necessity included more. There
were several "moments" in the life of Jesus, but it was not until they
were all past that the apostles could proclaim him as "Lord and Christ."
That is, the various events that had occurred as separate items of an historical sequence had to be seen for what they were—one divine act by
which God had reconciled man to himself. Similarly, the separate historical events by which God had both offered salvation to Israel and
prepared the way for Christ, have to be seen as moments in the one
divine act of man's redemption, as indeed the prologue to the Fourth
Gospel presupposes. . . . Just as the apostles at Pentecost saw for the
first time that the many events they had experienced with and through
Christ were but parts of one whole event which now became the content of their Good News, so they later came to see, as we may come to
see, that not only the events of Christ's own life are part of the divine
act of redemption, but that from creation one God has been working his
one gracious work.[10]

Now the ground of hope that the Ecumenical Reformation is real
reformation, "reformation according to the Word of God," is that
in this common listening to the Bible and learning that ultimately
it speaks a single Word—a Word which is not our word, and which
we never could have spoken or thought of for ourselves—the Church

is once again bringing itself under the authority of the Word. The Bible is again being given "free course" in the Church.

Again and again the Church, in its lack of faith, searches for a higher word than that which comes through the Bible. Sometimes we think we have found it: a word of philosophy, a word about "ideals," a word concerning the heroic and dauntless spirit of man. Then for a time the Bible is called on to illuminate and sanction this other word in such ways as we think we can compel it to do so. But soon or late—and is this not one evidence of the Bible's power?—we learn that this "higher" word is not higher; it is just our word. And the church that has only this really has nothing to say, for it has nothing to tell man that man is not quite able to tell himself.

For the preacher this reassertion of the Bible's authority is both bondage and liberation. The ministry is a life-long struggle against the temptation (how well some of us know it who have been preaching for any length of time!) to liberate ourselves from the Bible. We are always on the point of finding a better word to speak than the Word that speaks through this Book. Daniel Jenkins says:

[Many ministers] have felt it to be the purpose of their ministry to give gifts to their people out of their own spiritual treasury and to interpret to them the movement of the age, and have found the rigid limitation of the canon to be an intolerable fetter upon the freedom of their self-expression or their liberty to follow the zeitgeist wherever it might lead. It needs to be asserted against them that they are bound hand and foot by the canon, that the Gospel does not make sense unless the content and criterion of their preaching is the revelation of God in the Scriptures, and that their own sole freedom and title to minister consists in that bondage, because the salvation of their people depends on that bondage.[11]

Is there any of us who has not rebelled against this bondage? But it is only in the acceptance of it that true liberty of the Church's life and message can be gained. It is only by living in this "strange new world within the Bible"—the world in which God is really God —that we can live as the Church in this present world. It is only by the power of a different world that the Church can be extricated from its terrible immersion in the world of bourgeois culture. It is only by its at-homeness in this other world that the Christian community can live as not afraid of this present world—not afraid to immerse itself in its complexities and concrete issues and decisions. It is only by the power of a different world that the Church can be rescued from its fearful moralism, which is so afraid of the present world that it either succumbs to it or can do nothing but carp at it. It is only by the power of this other world that the Church can move out into the present world *as the Church*—the Church purged of churchiness; the Church really living an actual life of the body; a human community in every sense, but the true community, the true humanity, in which the image of God has been restored.

In this bondage to the Word we ministers are freed from the ultimate slavery of imagining that we are the saviours of men, and that it is our job to manipulate people's feelings and lives until they show what we regard as the signs of regeneration. We have the blessed liberty of knowing that it is this Word that saves, not we who try to speak so that *it* may speak to men's souls.

Reformation is possible when the Bible is given free power—when it stands over us as ministers and over the Church.* In a reformed and reforming Church it becomes impossible that an Innocent III should preach his consecration sermon simply about himself; or that we should preach about ourselves—our admirable ideas and original insights and noble ideals. With the Bible a free power the Church finds, as do its preachers, that its life is, as Barth says, "in dialogue." It is not left talking to itself.

* The fact that only in the Church is the Bible acknowledged as being Scripture does not lessen the force of this "over-againstness." *The Scots Confession* puts the matter incisively: "We affirm, therefore, that such as allege the Scripture to have no other authority but that which it has received from the Kirk, to be blasphemous against God, and injurious to the true Kirk, which always hears and obeys the voice of her own spouse and pastor; but takes not upon her to be mistress over the same" (Art. XIX).

The one great preacher in history is the Church. And the first business of the individual preacher is to enable the Church to preach. . . . He is so to preach to the Church that he shall also preach *from* the Church. That is to say, he must be a sacrament to the Church that with the Church he may become a missionary to the world.[1]

True preaching presupposes a Church, and not merely a public. And wherever the Church idea fades into that of a mere religious club or association you have a decay in preaching.[2]

The first vis-a-vis of the preacher, then, is not the world, but the Gospel community. The word is living only in a living community. Its spirit can act outwards only as it grows inwardly and animates a body duly fed and cared for. The preacher has to do this tending. He has to declare the Church's word, and to utter the Church's faith, in order that he and the Church together may declare them to the world. The Church may use, but cannot rely upon, evangelists who are evangelists and nothing else. When the preacher speaks to believers it is to build them up as a Christian Community. And the Church is built up by taking sanctuary, by stopping to realize its own faith, by the repetition of its own old Gospel, by turning aside to see its great sight, by standing still to see the salvation of the Lord.[3]

P. T. FORSYTH

CHAPTER III

The Word of the Church

IT IS in the light of the Ecumenical Movement that we are beginning to see the full import of P. T. Forsyth's words, nearly a half century after they were first spoken in the course of his Lyman Beecher Lectures. We are beginning to see what it means that the "one great preacher" is the Church, and that true preaching presupposes and requires a Church—not merely an audience, nor even the consciousness of individuals and communities to be evangelized. We are beginning to see what it means that the chief business of the individual preacher is to enable the Church to make its proclamation. (It is worth recalling, by the way, that the words quoted from Forsyth were spoken from the standpoint of English independency, which is frequently alleged to have a very casual and loose-jointed conception of the Church.)

For us as preachers there is a question that is prior to the continuously absorbing question of *what* to preach; and the answering of this prior question is indispensable to a valid answering of the other: it is the question as to *why* we preach at all. That there is a good deal of uncertainty in Protestantism today about the answer to this question is indicated by the frequent expression of two kinds of doubt—which may seem quite different on the surface yet take their rise in the same confusion of thought. From one direction come confessions of skepticism concerning the value and effectualness of preaching as such—as a means of accomplishing anything that is genuinely pertinent to the central concerns of Christianity. Even where this unbelief is not openly acknowledged, there are enough

signs of vagrancy of purpose and uncertainty of direction in some of
the preaching actually being done in the churches to suggest not
only a lack of definiteness concerning its objectives but a lack of
assurance as to the attainability of any objective at all. No doubt we
would agree that a good deal of contemporary preaching—even some
that gets into print—while it may be well organized logically, and
may display a certain attractiveness of literary style and illustration,
lacks the firm substantiality and penetrating thrust that come not
only from a clear understanding of mission but also from the confidence of being engaged in a mission which God intends, at least in
part by the employment of this foolishness of preaching, to accom-
plish.

Of another sort are the expressions of doubt not about the importance of preaching but about the availability of any genuinely "great
preaching" in the churches of our time. This so-called "great preaching" is seldom described with precision, but the names commonly
cited when this nostalgia is expressed give us a fairly good clue to
what is in mind.

These estimates of the place and character of the preaching office
—the one doubting the importance of preaching itself, the other believing in it but lamenting the want of "great preaching" today—
different and even opposite as they seem to be, are signs of the
same fundamental confusion as to why preaching is done in the
Christian Church—as to why we preachers preach at all.

For example, in one of the religious journals not long ago the
following news item appeared:

"I am through preaching sermons in either the conventional or popular sense of the word," wrote Dr. —— to the members of his congregation at —— Church, ——, California. "For some time I have felt a
dissatisfaction over the ineffectiveness of preaching." Instead, the minister told his congregation, he will for the next six months give from his
pulpit a series of "messages" on "How to Find Resources for Life's
Mastery." The minister explains that he is abandoning the traditional
sermon for a psychological approach to personal religious problems. . . .
His "no more sermon" program is being watched as an interesting experiment in the Christian enterprise.

One is tempted to make several comments on this announcement, of which three are particularly relevant.

First, most of us will recall that ever since we have been aware of such matters somebody has been calling for a "moratorium on preaching." Without a record of dates, one suspects that the call is sounded most frequently on Monday mornings—which may be a good sign. At times most of us preachers can heartily join Dr. Blank in saying that "for some time I have felt a dissatisfaction over the ineffectiveness of preaching"—our own preaching. In so far as the good Doctor's desire for change is due to this therapeutic discontent with his own past performance it is worthy of our approbation.

A second observation is that this "no more sermons" policy is not such a radical experiment as the news item suggests. Those of us who have been granted moments of realism in viewing our own work know that in the churches where we have preached there have been Sundays when no sermon or reasonable facsimile thereof was delivered. We have not noted that this involuntary—and we hope only sporadic—abandonment of the sermon has been attended by any remarkable access of spiritual vitality in the congregation. In a different category are some churches where the sermon seems to have been permanently—though surreptitiously—dropped from the service. There comes to mind a particular church bulletin board which invites the attention of the passer-by to the subject which is to be talked about on the following Sunday. The minister of this church evidently believes in what our California brother calls "a psychological approach to personal problems." We are invited to listen to addresses on "Help Yourself to Serenity," "Leave Your Worries at Church," "Religion Can Conquer Nervous Tension," "How to Face Trouble with a Smile," and "Christ's Formula for Success." In short, the topics suggest an unusually happy combination of the more fatuous sentiments of Henley's "Invictus" and Kipling's "If." Frequently the minister promises to deal with some variant of that enormously popular and profoundly Christian theme: "God Can Help You Relax." The abandonment of Christian preaching is not an altogether novel experiment for the church.

A third subject of reflection suggested by this news item is the curious distinction our California friend makes between the *sermon* (which he is now discarding) and this new and experimental form of address which he calls a *message*. One is a bit bewildered as to what he thinks a sermon is. Traditionally the burden of the preacher is, in the radical meaning of the term, just a "message." Not moralizing, not pious counsel, but a proclamation, an announcement, a "message"—about something done and something being done. As to what name should be used to characterize the ministerial talk based on "a psychological approach to personal religious problems" there might be some uncertainty. Some of the talks to which one listens strike one as being a skillful job of combining half-truths in such a way as to constitute a whole lie.

In any event, the frequent proposals for the abandonment of the sermon and the substitution of something else—possibly called a "message"—seem to me to indicate a good deal of uncertainty as to what Christian preaching is.

At the risk of being completely outrageous we might ask whether the plaintive cry for a restoration of "great preaching" may not be an expression of the same uncertainty. However, we might not go all the way with Daniel Jenkins, who writes as follows:

We do not always realize how much the so-called prosperous days of the late nineteenth and early twentieth centuries have affected the life of our churches. We often speak of them as the "great days," and of the personalities who dominated our pulpits and platforms as "the giants." In some ways they were truly great days, and none of us in the twentieth century dare deny that men of the calibre of Dale were giants. But the methods which some of the "giants" used in those days were such as to sap the spiritual vitality of our churches and to obscure their true witness. The cult of the pulpit "personality" and the "big occasion" and the "vast auditorium" had the effect of so titillating the palates of our people that they often ceased to be content with the plain, nourishing, unfailing food of the ordinary means of grace, and from being a true congregation they became an audience. Likewise [and here he addresses himself to Congregationalists concerning their neglect of the church meeting] the Church Meeting was frequently transformed from a responsible organ of Church government into a circle of devotees gathered round a "personality," who received every encouragement to become less and less a "painful preacher of the Word" and more and more a professional demagogue.

It is devoutly to be hoped that in the reconstruction of our church life . . . we shall take most of our inspiration from the seventeenth and the eighteenth centuries rather than from the end of the nineteenth.[4]

Whether or not we go all the way with this comment, we would probably agree that he is on the right road. Although there may be a place for "great preachers," that is not the vocation to which most of us are called. But there is a higher vocation to which we are all called, and that is to true and obedient preaching—true and obedient not merely to the conceptual content of the Gospel but to the nature and appointment of the preaching ministry in the Church of Jesus Christ. There will be in our preaching more of the quiet confidence and less of self-assertive straining after "results"; there will be a proper mingling—in Hendrik Kraemer's phrase—of "downright intrepidity and radical humility" when our exercise of the preaching office is set securely in the matrix of the Church. We need to understand in a more penetrating way what it means that "the one great preacher in history is the Church," and that our vocation is to enable it to preach. We need to consider what it means that Christian preaching is never without immediate awareness of this context—that it is always *from* and *to* and *by* and *for* and *with* the Church. That is not to suggest for a moment that the source of the Church's message is immanent in itself—that its message is not something "given" to it. As has been said, the Word of God is "over against" the Church; but it is the *Church* that the Word is "over against," and it is only in the Church that this Word is known to be God's Word. The Word is also "over against" all our human societies with their self-centredness and unfaith—over against them both in judgment and in mercy. But the Church cannot proclaim that "over-againstness" until it knows that the Word is over against itself.

Preaching, then, is in this fundamental sense Church proclamation. It is proclamation, first, to the Church from the Word, but from the Word that only the Church by the Holy Spirit knows to be God's Word. And it is, second, proclamation from the Church to the world.

Two comments follow. First, it is as Church proclamation that preaching becomes possible at all—that the preacher can preach without committing an act of insufferable arrogance. Second, because preaching is so bound up with the Church, very much depends on our understanding of what kind of reality the Church is.

A brief word is in order about the "possibility" of preaching.

To listen to some of us Protestants one would suppose that the Reformation took a wrong turning in its lifting up of the proclaiming of the Word of God. There is a feeling in some quarters that the sermon must be regarded as preliminary to, or a kind of postscript after, something else in the service that partakes more fully of the nature of the Church's worship. A recent dissertation casts about for some Protestant equivalent of the elevation of the Host in Roman worship—a kind of moment of epitome in which the manward movement of God's grace and the response of the worshipers in gratitude and adoration should be dramatically set forth. The writer fixes on the offering as such an act, suggesting that it should follow the sermon, and that the lifting up of the offering in dedication might be made the Protestant equivalent of the elevation of the Host.

Now it may be that a good case can be made by the liturgist for placing the offering after the sermon in the order of service; surely it ought to have some of the significance indicated by the author of this article. But what may well trouble us is the necessity for hunting about in odd corners of the order of worship to find something that might be as satisfactory a sign of the real presence of Christ as the central action of the Mass. Reformed theology is supposed to have long since settled this question for us. We *do* have our Protestant equivalent of the Roman elevation of the Host: it is the uplifting of the Word of God—the proclaiming and hearing of the Word. And it asserts a doctrine of the real Presence—presence not in metaphysical substance but in life and power. We believe that God in Christ is most really, most livingly, most personally present when He confronts the community of faith with His living Word. Indeed, for the Reformers preaching was the supreme sacrament of Christian worship. We may well question whether our Protestant preaching will be firmly grounded and deeply relevant until we recover this sacramental view of it. Sermon and what are commonly called "Sacraments" have essentially the same meaning. It was, in fact, a central concern of the Reformers to restore the proper and intimate connection between Word and Sacrament. It is not deprecatory of

Baptism and the Lord's Supper to call them "acted sermons"—proclamations. And the sermon is a spoken Sacrament. In all, it is the same Word—the Incarnate Word—that is given utterance.[5] And they are *Sacraments*, not "signs"—pallid word! As Sacraments they are not in the realm of sign but of event. They are not *the* event, but they may be the means to the event. "Like the bread and wine of the Holy Table," writes Lovell Cocks, "the words of the sermon are not themselves the sacrament, but 'elements,' symbols through which faith bears witness to the presence of the Incarnate Word." [6]

Moreover, the Sacraments are not fundamentally different from preaching. Says Lovell Cocks:

Baptism and the Lord's Supper are integral to the proclamation, for in these ordinances the Word is not only audible but visible, though only to the eye of faith. Here are acted sermons whose naked simplicity is a sign that our faith stands not in the wisdom of men but in the power of God. Here the preaching of the Church rises to heights beyond the summit of human eloquence, yet is preaching still. For the ordinances do not supply a grace lacking in preaching as such, but are rather seals that ratify the intention of the believing Church to proclaim no human surmise or opinion but the very Word of the saving God.[7]

Preaching has no meaning, any more than the other Sacraments, apart from the believing and witnessing Church.

And it is only as a Sacrament of the Church that preaching becomes possible at all for humble and self-critical men. When we "administer" the Sacrament of the Holy Table it is of course not from any worthiness of our own that we are permitted to do this, but because this Sacrament has been given to the Church, and the Church has in turn commissioned us to act in the Church and with the Church so that the proffering of this gift shall be continually renewed. So in our preaching; it is the Church's faith and the Church's acknowledgment that it must ever return to the source of its faith in the living Word that are the basis of our commissioning. We who are ignorant and sinful men are able to preach at all just because it is not we who preach but the Church—proclaiming and showing forth what it has been given.

When we recognize that the preaching ministry has significance only within the sacramental life of the Church, we are compelled to ask the deeper questions concerning the nature of the Church. And here the Ecumenical Movement, being engrossed in just these questions, can help us. In the nature of its central concern the Ecumenical Movement takes the fact of the Church with utmost seriousness. Perhaps that is why some of the ecumenical issues seem to us academic and even didactic—because some of us came to our maturity in a period when American Protestantism generally did not take the Church seriously. To understand what the ecumenical thinkers and study groups are saying to us, we have to understand their initial premise.

In the enterprise of ecumenical inquiry and conversation we do not see individual Christian thinkers discussing abstract questions of doctrine and polity. The Ecumenical Movement is first of all a concentrated effort of the Church to hear afresh the Word of God concerning herself—her nature, her mission, her order. The assumption that there *is* a Word of God addressed to the Church as a Church is perhaps the first thing that is meant by "taking the Church seriously."

To take the Church seriously means to see the necessity for the Church in the Gospel itself. It means to recognize that there is an indissoluble relationship between Gospel and Church. The two terms are not synonymous. The meaning of the Gospel is not exhausted in the Church. But the Church is a part of the Gospel. The Gospel cannot be stated at all without including in the statement a declaration that through the work of God in Christ there has been brought into being a new community, a new people. And this community is the Christian Church.

As one of the study commissions preparatory to the Faith and Order Conference at Lund concisely put it:

Koinonia, fellowship in the New Testament sense, is not something extra, but essential. It is not a coming together of private saved souls, but the way in which God reaches man.[8]

In suggesting that some of us have had difficulty in following the main course of ecumenical discussion because of the inadequacy of our own doctrine of the Church, it is easy to generalize too much from personal experience. Yet there seems to have been a common mood in at least one generation of theological students in what we sometimes call the liberal seminaries. We went into the ministry regarding the Church as a useful, perhaps necessary instrument— "necessary practically" as distinct from "necessary theologically"— though nearly always a reluctant and clumsy instrument for achieving ends beyond itself. We hoped it could be made roughly serviceable to these larger purposes if we could learn how to use it, and if we were careful not to become too much preoccupied with the ecclesiastical means and forgetful of the true ends outside the Church. We made much of the distinction between "Christianity" and "Churchianity." We conducted long and vehement arguments —and, perhaps, extremely irrelevant arguments—on the question whether or not Jesus intended to found a Church. We were fond of pointing to the fact that there was a large amount of social idealism and humanitarian service outside the Church and a large amount of complacency, smugness, and social reaction within; and we suspected that the members of the true Church of Christ might be as numerous outside the churches as among those listed on communicants' rolls. We took our stand with the prophets of Israel (so we imagined), and asserted our right to castigate the Church as the prophets had thundered against the ceremonialism and ethical emptiness of the religious cultus of their time. We were specially eloquent in accentuating the difference between the Church and the Kingdom of God, with the implication that we were disinterested servants of the Kingdom and would be faithful to this prior loyalty even at the cost of criticism and possibly the postponement of a raise in salary.

Where we found signs of virtue in the Church our approbation was likely to be given to its more peripheral and exotic features. For instance, some of us were fond of quoting a statement by a prominent minister who said that the Church provided the only free platform left in America. He said that in his own experience every other kind of organization had at one time or another warned him to avoid certain subjects. He had been cautioned—and occasionally threatened—by women's clubs, men's luncheon clubs, colleges, labor unions, veterans' organizations, associations of social workers—all of them. But on no occasion had an official of the Church attempted to tell him what he should or should not say. This statement by a prominent clergyman gave us great satisfaction; here was something good that could honestly be said about the Church. When occasion required us to give some sort of promotional talk and say a good word for the Church we could always fall back on this theme, "The Church as Defender of Free Speech."

With most of us this period of moralistic hyperthyroidism passed, and we had to recognize that not much was being accomplished by incessantly beating people over the head with a categorical imperative. Then we began to use the Church in the pursuit of other interests—aesthetic interests, for example. We started "enriching" the liturgy. We pushed around church furniture, moving the pulpit from the center to the right side, then to the left, and then to a spot midway between the floor and the rafters, and were surprised to discover that there was—to use a statistical term—no positive correlation between the location of the pulpit and the effectualness of the message proclaimed therefrom.

Or, if we were not aesthetically inclined, instead of rearranging chancels we tried our hand at rearranging people's complexes. We put notices in the bulletin stating that at such and such hours we should be available for "personal counseling." We were a little astonished when there was no sudden spurt of demand for our services, and that when people did come most of them seemed to want us to be just Christian pastors and seldom asked us questions about the emotional consequences of dietary idiosyncrasies in children. Since we had just read up on that subject we had to be content with working it into next Sunday's sermon.

Because preaching was not set firmly in an understanding of the Church and controlled by a sense of responsibility to the Church, the Gospel message was almost inevitably trivialized and sentimentalized. Ministerial drafts on the contents of The Reader's Digest were at least five times as heavy as their withdrawals from Deuteronomy.

Some of you will recall a series of articles in The New Yorker magazine about its phenomenally successful contemporary, The Reader's Digest. The tone of the articles was generally uncomplimentary and frequently derisive. One of the tricks of derision employed was that of comparing many of The Reader's Digest articles with sermons. Testimonials from ministers were quoted, saying that "The Digest is a veritable mine of sermonic materials." Passages that presumably were of great value homiletically were cited, and these were invariably sentimental. According to the author of these articles, the editor of another magazine accurately described the tone of The Digest in a terse sentence. Having been invited to luncheon with DeWitt Wallace, the publisher, he felt under obligation to become acquainted with his host's magazine. He bought a copy, read it through, and then made his comment: "Sounds like some damn preacher wrote it."

One did not have to read far in The New Yorker pieces to discern that their author brought to his work an anticlerical bias. Yet the fact that he found it not too difficult to make this identification—of the sermon with the saccharine, the sentimental, the egregiously moralistic—ought to give us pause.

The realization that preaching has higher and deeper dimensions than these, that its purpose is not adequately summarized as an essay on "The Most Unforgettable Character I Have Known" (even when that character is Jesus of Nazareth—which was for a while the real theme of liberal preaching) has pressed some of us back to the basic question behind all preaching. It is not the question, "What shall we preach?" for these other interests, aesthetic, psychiatric, moralistic, and so on, are not unproductive of subjects to talk about. It is the prior question, "Why do we preach at all?" And some of us have found the clue to the answer in recollecting that our ordination is to be ministers of the Gospel in the Church. Our ministry is the Church's ministry, and Gospel and Church are inseparable.

This has doubtless been brought home, at least in a general way, apart from the Ecumenical Movement, as a result of the vigorous biblical and theological study and reflection that have been going on in recent years in all sections of the Church. But in the Ecumenical Movement the issue has been sharpened. In the nature of that enterprise it has been necessary to try to fill what has been in modern times, in the phrase of Theodore Wedel, "The Great Vacuum in Christian Theology"—"Ours is, in some ways, the first age," he says, "called upon to formulate an ecumenical theology." And he suggests that "to work out a doctrine of the Church may have been a task assigned precisely to our era in Christian history." [9]

This task to which Wedel calls the Church is being insistently pressed in the Ecumenical Movement. As a result of asking together the fundamental questions about the nature of the Church, Christians from many traditions have agreed—with very few exceptions—that the Gospel sets forth, and at points where it is not explicit unmistakably implies, a "high" doctrine of the Christian Church.

We have come to understand that the Church must be seen as an intrinsic part of the story of God's redemptive action. It is inextricably a part of the whole event of Jesus Christ—the whole Christ; in Augustine's phrase, "totus Christus: caput et corpus." To set some abstracted and independent "Gospel message" in contradistinction to the Church in any simple way is to destroy this totality. It is to make the revelation consist only in those words and actions spoken and done by Jesus of Nazareth during the thirty years of his earthly life. But the wholeness of this event of Jesus Christ must surely include the ages that prepared for Him, the expectation and promise of His coming, and then, beyond this thirty years' span, the Resurrection, the gift of the Holy Spirit, and His living presence and action in the Church.

We have all come to recognize what has now become a truism in biblical study, that we are no longer permitted to draw a simple antithesis between the priestly and prophetic emphases in the Old Testament. It was on the basis of this false antithesis that a good deal of alleged "prophetic preaching" was done a few years ago. The assumption was that the prophetic standpoint, as contrasted with the priestly, was in some fundamental sense outside the Church and not responsible to the Church. By some of us it was construed as being primarily a position from which to castigate the Church, and as involving very little responsibility for building up the Church in faith and love.

It would be more nearly accurate, however, to say that the prophetic tradition was actually the "high church" tradition in the Old Testament community. The covenant relationship, the heart of the prophetic message, was not something to be proclaimed from outside the community with which this covenant had been made. Its very nature was that it had called into being a *people*. R. K. Orchard writes:

The word "covenant" might almost be taken as the epitome of the Old Testament message (especially the prophetic message). When used with reference to God it denotes not so much a mutual pact as a reciprocal relationship in which the initiative is on the side of God. When later ages referred to the relationship between God and Abraham as a "covenant," they were saying in effect that in that act God demonstrated that he actively controlled history, that he took the initiative in regard to a particular people and made them in a special sense the instrument of his will, and that their response made this possible. We have here, right at the start, the two great controlling certainties of Israel's religion, which are also the two great certainties of the Christian faith, that God is real, living, personal, active in history and known in his activity; and secondly, that he took the initiative and chose Israel to fulfil his purpose.[10]

We are coming to understand that only on the basis of what Orchard calls these "controlling certainties of Israel's religion" can we come to terms with the New Testament view of the Church. The meaning of the New Covenant is obscured, if not entirely obliterated, without its illumination by the Old Covenant and the significance of a people of the covenant.

The point is that for the prophets and for prophetic faith this community, the people of God, is central and normative in all their thinking and speaking. The members of the community, in their concrete historic life, repeatedly fall short of their calling and are guilty of infidelity. Then it becomes the prophet's stern duty to declare the judgment of God upon idolatry and disobedience. But always the judgment is pronounced in terms that are directly relevant to the nature and mission of the community itself. The people of God, in a very real sense, is judged by itself—not by standards immanent in its own life, but by what it truly and essentially is by the fact of God's choosing and His establishment of this covenant relationship.

So with the Church, as a part of the total event of revelation and redemption. As a new people it has meaning only against the background of the old people of God. It comes as fulfillment of the Old Covenant, but not as a natural or evolutionary fulfillment; the fulfillment is not logical but eschatological. The new community exists not as a result of continuous historical development but after death and resurrection. Yet it is dependent for the content of its meaning on the old community of Israel.

The Church is defined by C. H. Dodd as

the fulfillment of the prophetic eschatological hope for a new people of God. The Church is the New Israel which the prophets foresaw and foretold as the realization of God's redemptive purpose. The Church is Isaiah's Remnant. It is Jeremiah's People of the New Covenant. It is Ezekiel's Resurrected Israel, raised from the dead by the breath of the Lord. It is Daniel's People of the Saints of the Most High. It is Enoch's Congregation of the Elect. Throughout the New Testament runs this conception of the Church as the fulfilment of the prophetic eschatological vision and hope. The people of God, in the death and resurrection of Jesus Christ, have passed through death into newness of life.[11]

If a return to biblical sources presents us with a "high" doctrine of the Church, that is no less the result of an appeal to the Protestant Reformers. It is to be emphasized that this recognition of the necessity for the Church—in an absolute, theological sense, a necessity dictated by the nature of the Christian revelation—is from a Protestant standpoint a recovery, not an innovation. In the main line of Reformation thought, despite some recent vagaries of extreme individualism, there never has been any wavering from this high churchmanship. Surely Wilhelm Pauck is right in his courteous but insistent critique of Charles Clayton Morrison's Lyman Beecher lectures, *What Is Christianity?* at the point of Morrison's charge against the Reformers that they were responsible for what he calls the "Protestant heresy"—that is, the substitution of a concern for personal salvation in place of the community-character of the Christian faith. What has actually happened, Pauck remarks, is that the Reformers have been made responsible for an attitude that would have been repugnant to them and that has come into modern Protestantism through the influence of pietism and secular individualism. He says:

Dr. Morrison's major concern, namely the affirmation of the "historical" community-character of Christianity (Augustine stated it in the sentence: "Christ and the Church belong together") is sound, but it is regrettable that due to his misconception of the faith of the Reformation he has failed to see that in attacking the individualistic perversion of Christianity by modern Protestants he might have claimed the authority of the Reformers as his allies.[12]

The judgment of other competent scholars in a field that is now being worked very intensively, especially under the impetus of the Ecumenical Movement, sustains this verdict. The extreme individualism of the nineteenth century was not a working out of the implications of Protestantism but was an aberration of the Reformation faith.

Luther declared: "I believe that no one can be saved who is not found in this congregation [the Church]." "I believe that in this congregation, and nowhere else, there is forgiveness of sins." In his dispute with the Zwinglians he said that it is a dangerous thing to diverge from the faith of "the entire, holy, Christian church maintained harmoniously from the beginning, that is, for more than fifteen hundred years, throughout the whole world."[13] He renewed, of course, the New Testament emphasis on personal faith and decision. He said that "every man must do his own believing, just as every man must do his own dying." But he also said, to the comfort of the believer, that in the hour of his death all the angels and the saints, yea, the whole Church would be with him.

Calvin was no less explicit.

There is no other means of entering life unless the Church conceive us in the womb and give us birth, unless she nourish us at the breast, and watch over us with her protection and guidance. . . . Outside her bosom no forgiveness of sins, no salvation can be hoped for.[14]

In a later day, John Wesley declared that "the Bible knows nothing of solitary religion."

Last among these citations, as evidence that in the recovery of a high view of the Church Protestantism is reappropriating its central convictions, not engaging in innovation, we may note comments made by a group of British scholars who have recently written a very valuable tract as their contribution to the extraordinarily lively debate current among the Anglo-Catholics, the Evangelical party in the

Church of England, and members of the Free Churches. They call their tract *The Catholicity of Protestantism.*

The whole Reformation movement may be fairly described as an attempt to take seriously the New Testament doctrine of the Church, actual, visible and catholic, as the fellowship of the Holy Spirit, in reaction from the medieval neglect of the Church. This applies both to the Lutheran and Calvinist wings of the Reformation and also to the radical movement of the Anabaptists. No Reformation group can be justly charged with not giving serious thought to the doctrine of the Church, both from the point of view of theology and in its concrete expression. . . . Under the influence of secular liberalism and other forces there was a period of individualism in the nineteenth century which affected the life of the Church, and the effects of this have not entirely petered out in some sections of the Protestant communions. But this was a lapse from the Gospel, from which we have largely recovered, and we assert today the faith of the Reformers that outside the Church there is no salvation.[15]

The Ecumenical Movement, which, in the nature of its impelling motives and purposes, "takes the Church seriously," is giving to us ministers a deepened and heightened view of that community in which our ministry is set and apart from which it has no meaning. Just as it is impossible to converse about the Church in an ecumenical setting—to converse about its nature, its order, its unity— without taking the Church seriously, so is it impossible to preach the whole Gospel of Christ without taking seriously this community of the people of Christ, the mystery of whose calling, growth, and preservation through shame as well as glory is inextricably a part of the total event of God's redemptive deed.

Although we must not minimize the main points of misunderstanding and disagreement that remain, we are entitled to say that as a result of this ecumenical seriousness about the Church there is an impressive and growing consensus around some of the central issues. This is evident from the report of an American committee appointed by the World Council, representative of the major communions, which has been conducting a corporate study of the nature of the Church. Says the report:

. . . A broad and universal agreement lies in the very idea of the

Church itself as the people of God. It has been truly said that this is the most original aspect of our faith. Most religions have priests and temples, liturgies and codes of conduct, but the idea of the Church is characteristic of Biblical religion in which all Christian groups share in some way. All acknowledge one God as Founder of the Church. They recognize a covenant between a God who is faithful and a people whose faithfulness is ever overcome by him "whose mercy endures forever." The Church has been brought together by the revealing, redeeming act of God in Christ, whose purpose has its consummation in a redeemed people. . . .

What is the Church? It is the sphere of God's salvation in the present, and it is prophetic of his ultimate triumph in the Kingdom of God. It is constituted by the revelation of his grace in Jesus Christ. Its message is the gospel of redemptive love. It is marked by the presence of His Holy Spirit with all of its evidence of divine power. It is the people who have given allegiance to God in response to his gracious call. It is a body witnessing to his rule by their trust and obedience. This Church is set in the midst of a world where God's will is not yet done. The forms of organization exist to maintain its life and proclaim the message to the needs of men down the ages. They are simply earthly vessels which help to protect the heavenly treasure in the midst of the earthly task. But all of the branches must be truly united in order to witness to the rule of God in a Church Militant. For they all look forward to the Church Triumphant, which is the Kingdom of God.[16]

It is by and for and with and from this community of Christ's people that we are ordained to preach. The effect of that ordination is not so much that we are granted freedom of utterance as that we are set in a place of maximum responsibility—and not merely to the Word as individually apprehended but to the Word-in-the-Church. The message given to us is profoundly personal but not privately individual. It is not "truth through personality" in the individualistic sense, but truth in the corporate life of the fellowship. It is a message that we never could have received apart from the community and that never can be communicated to anyone else without the work of the Holy Spirit, whose sphere of operation is the Church. It is a message from and to the Church concerning the rule of Christ *in* the Church—a rule which, until it is known there, cannot be proclaimed to the world.

And it is finally the message of the triumph of Christ over the world through the Church. We are coming to see that our preaching concerning all this lacks depth without the profound eschatological note which has sounded so strange in the ears of Americans but to which we are compelled to listen in the ecumenical fellowship. If we are not yet prepared to understand the whole course of history eschatologically—though perhaps that is not as difficult as a few years ago—we can grasp some of its meaning in the situation of the Church. For how else can we understand the actual church militant except as a community living "between the times"—between Christ's appearing and His new appearing, between His Advent and the Parousia, between the time of His "I have overcome the world" and the time when all things shall be gathered up in Him, between the time of His victory and the time when the whole meaning of that victory shall be seen in a restored humanity and a new creation?

We crucified Him, but God raised Him from the dead. He is risen. He has overcome the powers of sin and death. A new life has begun. And in His risen and ascended power, He has sent forth into the world a new community, bound together by His Spirit, sharing His divine life, and commissioned to make Him known throughout the world. He will come again as Judge and King to bring all things to their consummation. Then we shall see Him as He is and know as we are known. Together with the whole creation we wait for this with eager hope, knowing that God is faithful and that even now He holds all things in His hand. . . . We do not know what is coming to us. But we know Who is coming. It is He who meets us every day and who will meet us at the end—Jesus Christ our Lord.[17]

The Church is called to live between possessing nothing and having all things. It has nothing in itself—nothing but the capacity it has been given to be addressed by God's Word; and the full purpose whereto that Word was sent is not yet accomplished. But the Church is also given all things, for that Word is Christ and He has come.

To proclaim the present and kingly rule of Christ in the Church, to build up the Body of Christ, and to extend the bounds of that community which in its triumph is the Kingdom of God—that is the purpose of the preaching ministry. That is why we preach. That is how we dare to preach. Not because we ourselves "have something to say," but because the Church has something to say and is commanded by its Lord to give the Word utterance, and because within the Church even our words may become the "elements" of a Sacrament that can "show forth the Lord's death"—and His power and victory—"till he come."

Division in the Church distorts its witness, frustrates its mission, and contradicts its own nature. If the Church is to demonstrate the Gospel in its life as well as in its preaching, it must manifest to the world the power of God to break down all barriers and to establish the Church's unity in Christ. *Christ is not divided.*

It is true that there are differences among us due to the various gifts and workings of the Holy Spirit within the one fellowship. But there are also differences among us which disrupt the Body of Christ, and separate us from one another. They spring from trusting in something other than the Cross of Christ.

We believe that through the ecumenical movement God is drawing His people together in order that He may enable us to discern yet more clearly the contradictions in our message and the barriers which are also hindrances to effective witness in a divided world. We can no longer be content to accept our divisions as normal. We believe that in the ecumenical movement God has provided a way of co-operation in witness and service, and also a means for the removal of much that mars such witness and service.

INTERNATIONAL MISSIONARY COUNCIL: WILLINGEN, 1952 [1]

CHAPTER IV

The Catholic Word

AMONG the most searching and disturbing documents in the chronicles of the Ecumenical Movement is one which for some reason has gained little notice. It is a resolution adopted in 1944 by the General Council of the Church of India, Burma, and Ceylon. It is so sharply relevant to the situation of the ministry in a divided Church that a fairly long quotation is in order. The statement will have its proper force if we recall that the Church of India, Burma, and Ceylon is an Anglican body, a portion of which, since the time this resolution was adopted, has joined with other denominations to constitute the Church of South India. We are to remember, therefore, that those who approved this statement were trained in a church tradition that cherishes a particular view of the nature of the ministry and the manner of its authorization. Against this background we may appreciate the measure of costly searching which must have preceded the drafting of this document.

We, the Bishops, Clergy and Laity of the Anglican Communion in India, Burma, and Ceylon assembled in Council at Nagpur have been burdened with a sense of frustration, as we have considered the failure of twenty-five years of effort to bring union to divided Christians in South India. But in this session there has been given to us a new vision of the unity of Christ's people and new hope as to the means by which that unity can be achieved. It has been laid upon us that we are still depending too much on human contrivance, and that we must learn to trust more fully in God's creative power to do new things and to give to His Church that unity which is according to His will.

We and those with whom we desire to unite are all one as members of the body of Christ, and through faith in the redemption wrought by God through His only-begotten Son, Jesus Christ; but so long as we remain out of communion with one another we are all defective in spiritual power. This is true in a special way of the ordained ministry. The ministries of all separated communions are by the fact of separation imperfect and limited in authority. As a result of this fact, the witness of us all to Christ is seriously compromised, and the work of setting forward God's purpose for the redemption of all mankind is grievously hindered.

We acknowledge that in the past we have failed in manifold ways to forward the work of reconciliation. For these sins of the past we earnestly repent and desire to atone; and we desire to express that penitence not only in words, but also in action. We believe that, when separated Communions come together again, their ministries should be united by a solemn act of humility and rededication, in which through the mutual laying on of hands with prayer they seek from God the enrichment of all those ministries.

If this method of achieving a united ministry commends itself to the mind and conscience of the Churches, those of us who are ordained ministers, bishops and presbyters, desire to present ourselves to those duly authorized in these Communions which are seeking to restore the unity of the body of Christ, that we may receive through the laying on of hands and prayer the spiritual endowment which in separation from them we lack.

We would earnestly commend this suggestion to our own Communion and also to other Communions who sincerely desire the union of the faithful, asking them to consider prayerfully whether this step is the will of God for us, and whether we may not hope by this means to be brought very much nearer to that perfect reconciliation and union which we all desire.[2]

As things turned out, this proposal was not adopted; doubtless it was deemed unnecessary as the plans for union took final shape. The scheme of union as later approved declared simply that all ministers of the uniting communions, upon acceptance of the constitution, should become ministers in full standing in the new united Church; therefore there remained no question so far as the newly constituted Church was concerned as to the equal standing and validity of the variously ordained ministries within it.

Yet one could wish that the suggestion had been followed.* There

* Something of this sort appears to be contemplated in the plan of

can be no more trenchant statement of the plight and problem of the ministry in a divided Church than this resolution from the Anglicans in India. Their proposal was made in the hope of removing the most stubborn obstacle to the South India union—as it has been the most perplexing area of difference in the Ecumenical Movement generally—that is, disagreement over the nature and commissioning of the ministry.[3] The declaration of the Indian Anglicans concerning the fundamental fact with which all constructive thinking must begin is of the highest importance: it is the fact that all ministries in a divided Church, however they may be constituted, are lacking in "validity." Every ordination is defective because, whatever the language and intention accompanying it, it is not in fact ordination to the ministry of the whole body of Christ. "The ministries of all separated communions are by the fact of separation imperfect and limited in authority."

Is there not accumulating evidence that this most resistant of all problems of Christian reunion, the problem of the ministry, will be resolved only when the churches approach it with this fundamental premise solidly in their thinking and conviction? The premise is that we are seeking the removal of a common defectiveness in our ministerial ordination. And this requires a common act of humility and obedience. It is far removed from the notion of reordination, for this common act of submission does not imply that any ministry has not been and may not be used of God as a channel of His grace, or that one ministry is more defective than any other. The proposed action would transcend some objections to the method of the extension of orders, such as is being considered in the conversations between the Anglicans in Canada and the United Church of Canada. For it is always possible that the meaning of this "extension," despite the precautionary language used in setting forth the Canadian proposal, may be construed invidiously and may be expressive of ecclesiastical

---

union now being developed in Ceylon. The proposed rite that is to complete the unification of the ministries of the uniting churches is not one of reordination, nor supplemental ordination, nor mutual commissioning. The central act in this contemplated rite is a prayer that God will complete and restore to wholeness whatever is partial and defective in the separate ministries that are to be consecrated to the service of the united Church.

pride; that is, it may lend itself to the assumption that one type of ministry is more truly a ministry of Christ than others, and that more is being "extended" from one side than from another. It cannot be denied that this view is strongly held by some persons, and any plan for providing a more widely authorized ministry will need to make room for this type of conscientious conviction. But the stoutest arguments in support of such a conviction somehow lose their invidious and offensive quality when they are preceded by a common act of contrition. Fellowship can be established and maintained among persons holding widely divergent theories of the nature of the ministry if we have all engaged in a common act of humility and have begun our discussion with an acknowledgment that all our ministries are defective as a consequence of our separation. The proposal of the Anglicans in India, that members of differently constituted ministries submit themselves to a mutual laying on of hands with prayer, seems to show how to take one long step toward unity. It is not reordination, nor does it carry the slightest implication of repudiating an ordination previously received. It is not extension of ordination—as though there were a different kind of grace conferred by different methods of ordination. It proposes, as the Anglican resolution happily phrased it, a mutual "enrichment" of all ministries.

Speaking as non-Anglicans—even as Congregationalists—some of us would aver that if there is an increment of grace—as there surely is— to be conferred by the prayer and imposition of the hands of a bishop, we should like to have it. For we need all we can get! We should have to recognize, however, that even this mutual enrichment of ministries would not complete our ordination, which would remain in some real sense defective until the wholeness of the Church itself is restored. But it would be, as has been said of the union in South India, "one small act of obedience to the recovered insight into the nature of the Body of Christ." [4]

We have been dealing with the defective character of the Church's ministry as a consequence of the Church's disunity. We must now proceed to confront the fact that the message of the Church proclaimed in the preached Word is also and for the same reason gravely disfigured. We cannot preach the Word of God in its fullness from our separated pulpits.

That statement will very likely invite some resentment. It may be made even more offensive if we add that if we resent it our case is even worse than otherwise, for it means that we are unconscious of the mutilated character of our testimony and are not engaged in the continuous critical effort necessary to correct it. We are obliged to recognize, further, that even the most rigorous critical work will not enable the Church to speak the whole counsel of God so long as it is disunited. For the order of the Church—or its disorder—is inevitably a part of the message of the Church. Some of the most damaging effects of our partiality may be lessened, however, when the Church engages in a strenuous enterprise of self-criticism. And the serious and responsible conversations among Christians that the Ecumenical Movement has done so much to bring about are the most fruitful kind of self-criticism in the Church's life today. They are the most thorough-going effort on the part of the contemporary Church to seek "reformation according to the Word of God."

It is important to note, further, that these conversations are dominated by an unremitting concern for the message of the Church. The discussions are not academic, though the language in which they are reported is sometimes deceptively technical. They have not centered on fine points of difference in biblical scholarship and theological interpretation. The focal preoccupation is kerygmatic. The participants are conscious of being entrusted by the Church with the vast responsibility of struggling with the question of the Church's proclamation. What is its message to the world—the one Gospel which, in our divided fellowships the churches declare in differing forms and in the accents of varied traditions, but which they are alike commanded by their one Lord to make known?

This is also, obviously and supremely, the preacher's question. The relentless and agonizing struggle with it is our primary business. No man has a right to go into the pulpit unless he is bruised from this struggle. All of us are worsted in it daily. No man is ever by his intelligence and learning a victor; for knowledge of this message and the power to speak it are always gifts of grace. But the marks of the conflict are far more valid insignia of the preacher's office than his clerical garb or his documentary evidences of ordination. It is a curious fact that some of the denominations that are most anxious

about the "validity" of the ministry are not always the first to sum-
mon their own ministry to the rigors of this warfare nor to offer them
help in the midst of it.

One important result of contemporary ecumenical labors is a
restatement of the fundamental character of the Church's message.
This in turn is a result of the ecumenical restatement of the underlying and all-important question of the nature of the Church itself.
Many of the controversies of the past have pivoted on the question
of the Church's essence. This form of the question is most often
introduced by those Protestant bodies that conceive their special
mission as the restoration of the primitive simplicity of the Church's
life. In making their protest against doctrines and practices that seem
to them unnecessary and confusing elaborations of the simple
Gospel and the natural, unformalized life of the koinonia, these
denominations have shown a tendency to define the essence of the
Church as the least that is required for the Church's existence. But
to be satisfied when the Church has been described in minima—or
its message formulated in minima—is like displaying as a clinical example of human life a person in whom pulse and respiration are reduced to the point of bare perceptibility. He is "alive"—but this is
not "life." In a crisis of illness we are thankful for these elemental
differentia between life and death, but we do not take them as
criteria of human existence in its fullness. In like manner we give
thanks that in the mercy of God the Church has been preserved
through days when the signs of its aliveness were reduced to faintly
discernible minima: the Word was heard, though almost without
understanding; the Sacraments were received, though with little
faith. Thus the "essential" Church was kept in existence; but it
was far from being the living Church.

The ecumenical conversations about the Church, as one hears
them today, are less preoccupied than formerly with defining the
Church in its essence, and more concerned about realizing the meaning of the Church in its fullness. To declare that where Christ is present—in whatever dim and amorphous intimation—there His Church
comes into being, may afford the consolation of knowing that the
Church will survive where even two or three have in their hearts the
faintest stirrings of faith and gratitude toward Him. But this comfort

ought not to be the standard of our churchmanship. In one sense, to say that the Presence makes the Church—especially when the discussion turns mainly on the sacramental mode of that Presence— may be to affirm that very little is required for the Church's exist- ence. But where Christians are truly aware of the Presence they will find themselves saying not "How *little* is essential," but "How *much* is required of us to whom much has been given." Where Christ is authentically present in the midst of His people they cannot be con- tent with any minimal definition of the Christian calling, message, and mission. The life of the Church is to be whole and complete: its worship is to be rich toward God, its faith resonant in confession and praise, its fellowship the joyous and liberating comradeship of those who share the secret that they have been forgiven, its ministry and mission as inclusive as the love of the Cross. Ecumenical thought to- day is not interested in the minima of the Church, but in its cath- olicity, its fullness.

The question of catholicity may perhaps be called the "great debate" in contemporary discussions of reunion. It is inevitably re- lated to the question of the Church's proclamation in preaching. As ministers of the Word we are commissioned to declare, not the irreducible minimum of the Gospel but the whole counsel of God. Partly as a consequence of brokenness in the Church that whole counsel is not set forth; both the Church and the world receive it only in fragments. As the ministers in South India sought a way to complete the authorization of their ministry, we have to find a new way through this problem. Let us attempt to state the issue.

All churches are agreed as to the central meaning and ground of catholicity. The fullness of the Church's life and message is Jesus Christ, the Incarnate Word. Where He is, there is the Church. This is the primary sense of catholicity.

It is the presence of the living Christ, recognized, adored, and obeyed, which secures the catholicity of the Church. Nothing else is necessary; and if a Christian in whom Christ dwells by faith lives on an island which is otherwise entirely inhabited by devil-worshipping savages, the catholic Church is present in his person, for he represents both his Lord and the people of his Lord.[5]

Moreover, all churches are bound to believe in and assert their own catholicity. In the nature of being churches they must believe that in their worship and proclamation, their Sacraments, their order, and their common life, they bear witness to Christ. And they bear witness not to some truth about Him but to His total presence and lordship. Oliver Tomkins says:

No church worthy of the name has ever thought of itself as "embodying a valuable emphasis." A living Church is one that believes that it offers, not a fragment of the Christ, but the whole Christ. Yet, paradoxically, the renewal of the Church involves each part of the Church acknowledging that, although it should offer the whole Christ, it does not offer a whole Christ to men because men are not offering a whole Church to Christ. The whole Christ is latent in every part of a divided Church, but the whole Christ is only patent in a united Church. The whole is truly present in every part when the Church is undivided, for Christ is not divided and where Christ is, there is the Church.[6]

The situation among the churches is that churches affirming catholicity and deeply believing it of themselves are unable to recognize it in other communions. Yet neither can they wholly deny it. This far we have certainly come. The churches are bound to recognize in one another, in some very real sense, the presence and work of the living Christ. And where Christ is, there is His Church. We are able to recognize Christ's presence and lordship in the churches, but the churches are not all able to recognize one another as being in the Church. It is the paradox and tension of this situation that generates the longing and endeavor toward full union. As Amsterdam put it:

Although we cannot fully meet, Our Lord will not allow us to turn away from one another. We cannot ignore one another, for the very intensity of our difference testifies to a common conviction which we drew from Him. The Body of Christ is a unity which makes it impossible for us either to forget one another or to be content with agreement upon isolated parts of our belief whilst we leave the other parts unreconciled.[7]

And Evanston added:

To stay together is not enough. We must go forward. As we learn more of our unity in Christ, it becomes the more intolerable that we should be divided.[8]

What is the basis of this withholding of recognition—that is, recognition by the churches of catholicity, of the fullness of the Church, in one another? Amsterdam tried to state the major separation as between "catholic" and "protestant" (or "evangelical") conceptions of the Church. Admitting that it was impossible to do justice to either conception, especially by setting them in opposition, the report found certain general marks of distinction. The "catholic" view "contains a primary insistence upon the visible continuity of the Church in the apostolic succession of the Episcopate." The "protestant" conception "primarily emphasizes the initiative of the Word of God and the response of faith, focused in the doctrine of justification *sola fide*. But," the report goes on to say, "the first group also stresses faith, and the second also stresses continuity of the visible Church in some form." [9]

It has become apparent since Amsterdam that there is a great deal of dissatisfaction with this attempt to state the main line of difference. Indeed, in the discussions of Section I, which drafted this report, there was an effort to include a characterization of at least one other type of emphasis—namely that of the "gathered Church," "the community of the Holy Spirit." President Van Dusen has recently strongly expressed a conviction that the World Council discussions should return to the premise of both Lausanne and Amsterdam, that there are "three major conceptions of the Church and of normative church order, which may be roughly designated episcopal, presbyterian, and congregational." [10]

What is even more difficult and confusing is the fact that across these principal lines of division are many areas of agreement as well as difference, and that *within* these major divisions are many matters of sharp divergence as well as consent.

This is not only clear from the statements of theologians and church leaders, but is a matter of commonplace experience with all of us. In the United States, especially, the lines of demarcation between one type of denomination and another have become so blurred that one may ask whether the discussion of problems of ecumenicity and church union in terms of the traditional classification of Christian bodies—even the three, episcopal, presbyterian, and congregational—has not become quite unfruitful if not disastrously misleading.

Where are "pure" examples of any of these Church types to be found? Every one of the denominations possessing the minimal amount of ecumenicity requisite to joining in the program of Protestant co-operation—every one, for example, holding membership in the National Council of Churches—has appropriated to itself elements of all three of these systems. To conduct the ecumenical debate on the basis of the traditional nomenclature is to confront people with problems and choices that frequently, in the way they are stated, have no substance in reality. And that is to make more difficult a clear-sighted approach to issues of mutual recognition and union.

When some Congregationalists object to a plan of union with the Evangelical and Reformed Church on grounds of its being "too presbyterian," they are simply standing in the way of any imaginative appraisal of its possibilities—any sharp look at the proposal in its concreteness, and with a reasonable assumption that its skeletal mechanics will be clothed by Christian courtesy, forebearance, and charity. Similarly, when a Methodist bishop airily disposes of a plan of union which several denominations are discussing, by saying that it is "too congregational," he is arresting thought by the intrusion of an epithet. In what specific ways is it "too congregational"? Does it make too large a place for the local congregation? Or does it not make a large enough place for a Methodist bishop?

Even when episcopacy is brought forward as the *sine qua non* of any comprehensive movement toward union, and by that fact becomes at the same time an apparently insuperable barrier, we have to ask, "What kind of episcopacy?" When the Archbishop of Canterbury is willing to propose that non-episcopal communions experiment with episcopacy after their own fashion, and, as he put it, "try it out on their own grounds"—a phrase the Anglo-Catholics must have found more revolting than using "fellowship" as a verb—one suspects that even the Archbishop views the concept of episcopacy as being very elastic.

This blurring of the lines of denominational and confessional distinction is one of the most obvious facts to anyone acquainted with any considerable segment of American church life and thought. There are Presbyterian churches that are more cantankerously congregational than most Congregational churches—and Congregational churches more rigorously Calvinist in their theology and discipline than most Presbyterian congregations. There are ministers of allegedly "nonliturgical" denominations who are more self-consciously and maniacally liturgical than any Episcopalian or Lutheran of my acquaintance. There are even Episcopalians whose respect for bishops is almost as microscopic as that of Congregationalists, say, for denominational secretaries.

Yet, as Amsterdam pointed out, despite this blurring of distinctions when any detail of faith and practice is considered alone, each of these major views of the Church is a totality.

Each of these views sees every part of the Church's life in the setting of the whole, so that even where the parts seem to be similar they are set in a context which, as yet, we find irreconcilable with the whole context of the other.[11]

One further observation—and this is an intentional complication of this picture of confusion, in the conviction that the very confusion is full of meaning. The perplexity of the present situation is emphasized when we try to state what we see in one another's life that is truly of the Church of Christ. When the Central Committee of the World Council, meeting in Toronto, is able to issue a statement recognizing that there are some marks of the Church to be discerned in all communions, that is doubtless something. But when the Central Committee expresses this truth in the form of an acknowledgment that the member churches of the World Council are agreed in recognizing in one another "vestigia ecclesiae," one is impressed by the evidence that somebody knows Latin, but one wonders whether the spirit of ecumenicity is greatly served by it. Evidently this was the maximum affirmation around which agreement could be gathered at the time. But would it not have been better to wait and pray until something more could be said? As Clarence Tucker Craig remarked concerning the statement:

I do not feel gratified when some other church grudgingly admits that vestigia ecclesiae are to be found in the church through which God's forgiving grace was mediated to me.[12]

What can be meant by such a statement? One's first feeling is that it must mean either that someone on the Committee has exceedingly intractable convictions about church order, or that in some quarters the World Council is facing forms of ecclesiastical arrogance that are considerably more than *vestigia*. *Vestigia*, indeed! Let us have some vestiges of charity and some vestiges of humility.

There are probably no methods of analysis by which the relative proportions of genuine conviction and insufferable arrogance necessitating such a phrase can be ascertained. Like the membership of the true Church, the nature of this mixture is known only to God. Since the arrogance cannot be separated and held up as an object either of ridicule or of penitence, it has to be dealt with in some other way. Perhaps it can be by-passed and allowed to wither on the vine. The process of withering will be hastened if the vine is not watered by tears of self-pity shed by those of us who belong to "vestigial" churches.

Walter Marshall Horton has urged the need for a clear statement of acceptable terms of church union from the side of the so-called Free Churches—since the setting of conditions is generally done from the "catholic" side.[13] Perhaps the mildness of enthusiasm from some of us for that proposal is due in part to reticence about the use of the name "Free Churches"—a name which, in America at any rate, is bound to be somewhat invidious. But we might agree with him to the extent of saying that there ought to be less of an attitude of waiting for somebody else to relax—an attitude that sometimes must give the impression of lack of seriousness—among us whose views of church order are less susceptible to charting and formalizing than the views of some other bodies. We need to make it clear that while we are not legalists as regards the *form* of the Church, we are as serious as anybody about the *fact* of the Church and about its divine establishing and sustaining. We are as serious as anyone about the *order* of the Church, as the Church's obedience to its Head. And we need to make it clear that churches in which men and women have made the response of living faith, have been constant in prayer, and rich in the fruits of the Spirit—and in which we ourselves have received the Gospel—are not to be reduced to *vestigia*. No doubt a certain steady pressure of insistence on this matter of recognition is necessary in the Ecumenical Movement today.

It is a curious fact that the churches which profess the greatest devotion to catholicity, and labor most assiduously to define and list the conditions of fullness of life and witness, seem often to drift farther away from catholicity of spirit and practice the more they are concerned about it. Is it because in this work of refinement and definition their attention is focused more and more on secondary characteristics, and thus they become less able to recognize in other churches the primary characteristic of catholicity—the presence of Christ in His Lordship over the Church?

It was in part because of the uncatholicity of Roman Catholicism that the Reformation occurred. The reformers sought to restore not only the inner purity of the Church but its true catholicity. John McNeill says:

> The Reformation was a revolt, not against the principle of unity and catholicity, but against the privileged and oppressive monarchy of Rome —an uprising not merely of national, but of catholic feeling, against what had become an overcentralized imperialism in Christianity, which made true catholicity impossible. . . . The parish was not a congregation, but an administrative unit. The governmental aspect of unity was not supported by an adequate religious bond. The Roman Church had substituted the idea of "Roman obedience" for the earlier conception of catholicity expressed in a universal free communion. . . . In the Reformation the Christian people were taught to think, to believe, and to sing together, and given a new vision of the high and universal fellowship which is the church catholic.[14]

A preoccupation with the formal aspects of catholicity—an endeavor to list exhaustively the elements necessary for the fullness of the Church—seems, as has been pointed out, to result in dulling the capacity to recognize catholicity in others. This is true not only of the communions that hold to the general conception the World Council calls "catholic." The more radically "protestant" bodies, perhaps most often in a negative way—by listing the things that in their view do not belong to the Church's real life—may be quite as uncatholic. From wherever we view the problem, the same tendency is at work. Other churches, seen from outside, are recognized as "embodying a valuable emphasis"; while our own church, known from the inside, obviously endeavors in its worship, testimony, and common life to offer men the whole Christ.

Thus Father A. G. Hebert acknowledges that in the early Church there was recognition of what he calls "the congregational principle."

[In the local congregation] there is personal contact and love and fellowship existing between the members, [and] the unity of Christians with one another can here become a living reality. Here lies the partial truth of the Congregational conception of the Church, in which it has been truly seen that the whole mystery of the Church is present in each local part.[15]

These words are from an Anglo-Catholic scholar. It may be assumed that the ascription of "partial truth" to the congregational view is not intentionally condescending and was written ungrudgingly. This characterization, as Father Hebert has stated it, is perhaps all that a Congregationalist should wish to claim—that there is a "partial truth" in this testimony that the Church is truly present in the local fellowship of believers—that the local church is, in P. T. Forsyth's phrase, "the outcrop there of the total and continuous Church, one everywhere." In fact the Congregational fathers of the seventeenth century never claimed that this was anything more than a "partial truth." Many Congregationalists would grant, moreover, that the competence of the local congregation to be fully the Church in a particular place can be realized in forms other than those traditionally congregational.

But Father Hebert should remember that when the early Congregationalists set out to embody in their church life this "partial truth" they did not consider that theirs was a "partial Church." They believed that the whole Christ was present in it. Their faith was the catholic faith. They established a church order and discipline, centering in the church meeting, so that Christ might rule in His Church. They established synods through which they sought to know Christ's will for the churches. Their separation from the Established Church, undertaken with infinite regret, was not for the purpose of starting a church of the partial truth but for the recovery of a part of the whole catholic truth that had been obscured or denied.

This blindness that results from the withholding of recognition of at least the "latent" catholicity of other churches, becomes most disastrous when Father Hebert deals with the question of the ministry. His fundamental contention is that Free Church ministries, though in some sense authentic ministries, are nevertheless different from the catholic conception of the ministry, grounded in the "principle of succession." He writes:

The Church of England intended to retain the Ministry which had always existed from the days of the Apostles. . . . The Free Churches believed, each in its own way, that faithfulness to the Gospel required them to make a fresh start; and each had a vision of some element in the Apostolic Ministry which current Catholic practice had obscured. The Presbyterians saw the importance of the ancient college of elders; the Independents saw the local congregation as the local embodiment of the Church Catholic; and the Baptists added to this the knowledge, shared by every foreign missionary, that the original and normal type of baptismal rite is adult Baptism; the Methodist "classes" existed to provide for a live and active laity.[16]

So far one may generally agree with Hebert; though one must resist the implication—if it is there—that these ministries existed mainly to "make a point," so to speak—a doctrinal or ecclesiastical point— and not to be full ministries of Jesus Christ in His Church. But Father Hebert goes on to suggest that in a clear recognition that these Free Church ministries are fundamentally different from the Catholic ministry may be found the starting-point for plans looking toward union. He then gives a specific illustration, and we begin to see what he is driving at.

The Methodist minister is not and never has been the same thing as the Vicar of a parish church; he was once, and may become again, the leader of a religious society within the congregation, going to the parish church for the sacraments. This case is seemingly, but perhaps not really, less difficult than that of the older Free Churches, which stood for a rival form of church polity. . . . No advance here is possible till we have reached some common understanding of the nature of the Ministry. But it may be worth while to recall that some of our parish churches still have endowments for a "lecturer," dating from Puritan days; and these might be used again in a less polemical spirit.[17]

It seems a pity that this should be the conclusion and climax of what is in many ways a discriminating, irenic, and even generous book. Father Hebert seems to be saying that the differences of ministries shall be assimilated into a united Church through the establishment of functional suborders. What he calls the Catholic Ministry remains the true ministry of the whole Church. The Methodist minister becomes the leader of a "religious society" within the local congregation; the Congregational or Presbyterian minister becomes a lecturer on some sort of ecclesiastical foundation. One feels a maddening sense of frustration when a serious attempt to discuss "the form of the Church" comes to nothing more than this.

We have noted that the very confusion of this problem of catholicity—of recognizing the Church in the churches, and the churches as being in the Church—has a positive meaning and affords ground for hope. It means that we are driven to find a new approach—not by any means a totally new approach, for I am sure that it is implicit in much that has been done, and it derives from experiences of the Church that are much older than the modern Ecumenical Movement. The specific steps to be taken are not entirely plain, and will become so only as we begin actually to walk; but we can see the direction we are required to go.

How shall we proceed to reappropriate that fullness of the Church's life that only the "whole Christ" can give—which every church affirms in principle it is able to receive but that in some very true sense (and because we know it we are not permitted to rest) is denied to all of us in our separation?

The method by which catholicity is to be sought is not, everyone is now agreed, the method of synthesis—trying to fit varying points of view and practices into a logical new pattern, forgetting that these points of view and practices become something different—and nearly always something enfeebled and bloodless—when they are separated from the whole to which they belong. The ecumenical method—which Henry P. Van Dusen calls "the method of comprehension"—does not seem entirely satisfactory. He discusses this method primarily in relation to church practice, especially as regards baptism, the Eucharist, and the ministry. The argument is this: In church practice there has always been and is today variety. We must assume that this variety cannot be wholly due to error or sin. Unity, therefore, he says, "should envision the inclusion of persistent variations, stripped, so far as may be, of their accidental or willful extravagances, but without loss of the essential validities testified to by origin, historic persistence, present fruitfulness." [18]

Certainly we have no quarrel with the purpose here envisioned, but we are forced to some questions about method. How do we decide whether a practice is "persistent"; how long must it have been followed in some section of the Church? How, especially, do we get at this business of "stripping" our varied practices of "accidental and willful extravagances"? By what standard are we to determine what these are? There are persons who regard the insistence of a Congregational church on calling its own minister as an accidental and willful extravagance. Others—even some Methodists—regard a Methodist bishop as an accidental and willful extravagance! The problem is to find some norm for discriminating between valid and enriching variety and whimsical or prideful extravagance.

The ecumenical method, as it has actually been developed and employed, is of another sort. It is not synthesis. It is not comprehension. It is what was really proposed by the Anglicans of India concerning the ministry. It is the method of *resubmission*. It is the resubmission of the *whole* of the Church's message and life to the giver of its message and life—the living Word of God. To construe this as merely a return to biblicism and a starting all over again of the controversies and schisms due to the different ways men read the Bible is to misunderstand it completely. The fact that the churches are reading that Bible together and in a new way makes one very great difference; the fact that they are reading it not to justify their separations but to be led to overcome them makes another very great difference. And the fact that this normative Word is a *living* Word —which speaks to us in our *present* experience of conversing, studying, praying, listening, repenting, and hoping together—makes the *supreme* difference.

A group of Anglo-Catholic scholars have recently given us a statement on *catholicity* with much of which those who do not share their ecclesiology will find it difficult to agree. But they are surely right when they say:

In so far as progress has been made towards a synthesis in recent years
[we may regret that word, but it is there] it has been made, not by exer-
cises in Highest Common Factor, but by going behind the rival doctrines
to something which they all, in various ways, misrepresent.[19]

It is this "going behind" that is the essence of the ecumenical
method. And it is a "going behind" in the assumption that our
separate and rival testimonies do in fact misrepresent that to which
they testify. The starting point may well be the cultivation of a
common skepticism regarding every form of traditionalism—especially
regarding our own. This is not to minimize the importance of living
tradition, from which every church inevitably and rightly draws
vitality. The difficulty is that no denomination can be certain of its
own power to discriminate between valid tradition and mere traditionalism—the perpetuation of accustomed ways simply because they
are ours, and without submitting them to fresh examination in the
light of the Gospel.

What is needed is a common acknowledgment, thoroughgoing
and drastic, of an incompleteness that characterizes all our churches
and ministries. When an Anglo-Catholic states his conviction that
the church to which some others of us belong and the ministry to
which we have been ordained are "essentially incomplete" we may
agree with him. But we could bring more warmth and grace to the
agreement if he were willing to consider the possibility that what he
says of our church and our ministry is also true of his own. This is
precisely what the Anglicans of South India were able to say; and
their saying it made all the difference between abandonment and
continuation of effort at a critical juncture in the union negotiations.

They proposed as a means of reconciling differences over the ministry that the ministries of the uniting churches submit themselves
to one another and to the Lord of the Church in an act through
which they should seek from God an "enrichment" of all their
ministries. There was no doubting of the reality of existing ministries. There was no calling in question the validity of the ministries
of their spiritual fathers from whom in varying ways they had received ordination. The proposed act was appropriate at any time to
any ministry; for what is the ministry if it is not a submission and
continuous resubmission to the authority of the Word in Christ?

The proper name for this method is "reformation according to the Word of God." And the real division among the churches is at this point—whether they expect and pray for renewal (and for the unity that can come only through that renewal) to be wrought in this way. Does the Church seek the fullness of Christian witness and life somewhere within itself—in something that it already has—in its tradition, its continuity in time, its sacramental practice, its order? Or does it look for that fullness through resubmission of itself to the regnancy of the living Word of God?

In concrete terms, this means that there is need for intensifying the church union efforts of the Ecumenical Movement, and in a somewhat narrowed area, without in any way diminishing the work toward understanding over the whole range of that Movement in its present form. The intensified efforts toward union would be undertaken by churches that genuinely accept the principle of reformation according to the Word of God. We should find that this acceptance transcends the "catholic"—"protestant" division.

We have to face the fact that outside this principle not only is union far off but real conversation is not now possible. There is only monologue. The communions which hold that in their existing life and form they already possess full catholicity—that it can become "fuller" only in the sense that more of us may come to see it their way—are bound by conviction to an attitude in which no real listening is possible. They can only try patiently to explain, and wait for the rest of us to see the truth. When they look for a new event to occur in the Church it is an event that will happen to us. When they pray for reformation of the Church it must necessarily be a prayer that we shall be reformed. We need that prayer, and join them in offering it, and hope that God will use it to make the thing happen; but it is not the Church Universal praying for its radical remaking.

What is suggested here does not mean a cessation or lessening of fellowship and effort toward understanding through the whole membership of the Ecumenical Movement. We have to thank God for the mystery—and it is a mystery—that Eastern Orthodoxy is in that movement. We have to thank God for the mystery that the Anglo-Catholic party has remained within Anglicanism. We ought to be specially thankful—and hopeful—because of the wonderful resurgence of biblical interest and study in all branches of Catholicism, and for the genuinely vigorous work in biblical theology that some of the Anglo-Catholic scholars are doing.

But a different kind of approach to one another is possible, and an immediate hope is justified, among those churches that genuinely accept the method of resubmission and reformation according to the Word of God. Questions of theological view, of confessional formulation, of sacramental practice, of Church order, become not "open questions" in the sense that we bring to them no depth of conviction, but fundamentally new questions, in the sense that together, in the authentic corporate life of the Ecumenical Movement, we submit these questions, together with ourselves, in faith, to change —real renovation—by the living Word.

Where this is possible we dare not wait; it is not only the hope of union but the hope of that sweeping and all-pervasive reformation of the Church's life that is so clearly needed if the Church is to be in truth the restored humanity capable of mediating life to a dying world.

The issues we have been discussing in this chapter may seem to be problems of ecclesiology in the more technical meaning of that term, and therefore problems that have little connection with the work of preaching. There are at least two points, however, at which they bear directly on the preaching office.

First, it is to be noted that the preacher himself—the minister—is in a uniquely sensitive and responsible position vis-a-vis the ecumenical problem. In a peculiar way he is the ecumenical problem. He embodies and personalizes that problem. Whenever he stands before his congregation he represents, not in some abstrusely theological sense but in visible form, both the ministry of the whole Church of Christ and the tragedy of the Church's separations. He is called and appointed to be a minister of Christ, and Christ is one. But his ministry is not acceptable to the whole people of Christ— neither as a ministry to themselves nor on their behalf to the world.

What minister can read without true penitential sorrow that section of Van Dusen's discussion of The Issues of Christian Unity in which he dwells on the minister's status as the most recalcitrant factor in the whole complex of divergent theories and practices? Van

Dusen enters into the imagined reflections of a non-Christian observer watching the efforts of churchmen to heal their divisions. The bystander notes that the gravest difficulties preventive of union are not around doctrines concerning God, the world, man, Christ, salvation, and other concerns that are commonly regarded as having primary theological importance; the most serious disagreements have to do with the Church's view of itself. And among these the most stubborn and irreconcilable pertain to the Christian ministry, its origin, ordination, and authority. The author follows his imaginary observer in noting further that the overwhelming majority of the Churches' spokesmen at any ecclesiastical gathering or on any theological commission are clergy, and then asks:

Might he not be struck by the fact that the single point which, according to their confession, prevents the unity of the Church concerns what those who are charged with perpetuating or healing the Church's divisions—the ministry—believe about themselves? Might he be tempted to the conclusion that what is required for the unity so fervently espoused is not so much additional argument or further light as downright conversion, conversion of the ministry? [20]

This problem of the minister, as the most refractory element in the whole ecumenical process, inevitably has an effect on his preaching. Whenever he enters the pulpit, even if he never alludes to questions of Christian unity, he stands there as a negative witness. As a minister he represents a chief obstacle—perhaps the chief obstacle—to the Church's unity. Since he cannot in the midst of our present divisions escape this role, a question of major importance is how he bears himself in it. Is he complacent in this position, or uneasy? Since he is by virtue of his office a walking epitome of the ecumenical problem, does he show signs of being concerned about its solution? Compelled to occupy an obstructionist position, is he visibly embarrassed about it? Some clue to his attitude will certainly appear in his preaching.

Thus the minister's own predicament may be the most appropriate starting point for effective ecumenical teaching.

There is in his dilemma, for example, a key to the right kind of confession and penitence for Christians as they face the meaning of their divisions. Some of the admissions of sin that are heard in ecumenical gatherings have an unreal and sentimental—even a mawkish—quality. Whose sins are we confessing, after all, and what kinds of act and attitude do we have in mind as sinful? Are we offering penitence in behalf of our forefathers, some of whom when they separated themselves from other Christians did so with vast regret, and only at the instance of the deepest and most fervent conviction that they were acting in obedience to Christ? Are we to repent for their sincerity? Are we to be penitent because we also have convictions in matters of faith and order, and because there is not yet enough wisdom among Christians to see how these can be reconciled and held in a comprehensive unity with other convictions to which other Christians cleave with like earnestness? Depth and genuineness of conviction do not seem the most suitable occasions for contrition. As one of the Evanston statements tersely put it, "Penitence cannot be hypocrisy."

The nature of the repentance to which Christians are called as they confront their divisions is well symbolized by the predicament of the minister. He is at once a perpetuator of the ecumenical problem and a principal agent in attempts at its solution. Ministers meet in ecumenical gatherings, find that the most perplexing issues of unity have to do with their own ministry, and fail to resolve them. But these same ministers keep coming back to hold more conferences! They fail, but they cannot rest in their failure.

In this situation the acknowledgment of failure, the cry for help, and the humble pledge of willingness to receive mercy and new leading as God gives them to us, are the ingredients of sincere penitence. This is not to minimize the existence of recognizable and specific sins of pride and self-will. One of the results of the ecumenical encounter is the acquisition of skill in an enterprise of self-criticism that is increasingly precise and incisive in identifying these sins. Yet the core of the ecumenical dilemma is just that we cannot agree—and we cannot agree because we actually do not know—which of our convictions represent sinful pride of tradition and opinion, and which are expressive of unconditional loyalty to Christ. Evanston said:

True repentance is the acknowledgment before God that we have

sinned so as to be caught in the net of inexplicable evil and rendered unable to heal our divisions by ourselves. But we cannot in sincerity and
truth repent of our various understandings of God's will for His Church,
unless the Spirit Himself reveals that our understandings have been in
error. . . . The point at which we are unable to renounce the things
which divide us, because we believe that obedience to God Himself
compels us to stand fast—this is the point at which we come together to
ask for mercy and light. So what we believe to be our "faithfulness" must
bring us together at the foot of the Cross. The Cross tells us that where
the dividing power of sin was most manifest, there God has gained the
victory.[21]

The point is that one of the best ways for the minister to communicate to his people the nature of the ecumenical problem and
task may be in terms of his own predicament. It is becoming increasingly urgent that the members of our churches shall be informed
about these issues—first, as a matter of responsible churchmanship,
and second, to be prepared to explore specific opportunities for union
that will present themselves with growing frequency. The people of
the churches need to see something of the intricacy of these issues,
as a safeguard against false expectations of quick and facile solution;
and something of their Christian momentousness, so that they may
be patient and persistent in support of continued efforts to find a
way through. The minister in his own dilemma brings these facts
into high visibility.

He is ordained, in principle, to the catholic ministry, for every
church in one way or another makes this claim for its ministry.
Ordination is a commissioning for the service of Christ's whole
Church, not just a fragment of it. This is generally true even of the
most radically independent bodies, in which ordination is by and for
the local congregation alone. Even here is an implicit affirmation of
catholicity, for in this view the local church is all the church there is.
More often than not, however, the churches that lay greatest stress
on local autonomy go beyond this implicit claim and affirm an explicit doctrine of catholicity for their ministry. Says a statement approved by the Council of the Baptist Union of Great Britain and
Ireland:

Many among us hold that since the ministry is the gift of God to the Church and the call to exercise the functions of a minister comes from Him, a man who is so called is not only the minister of a local Baptist church but also a minister of the whole Church of Jesus Christ.[22]

Here then is a claim to catholicity that nearly every church asserts for its ministry. Yet no church is able to make good the claim in face of the incontrovertible objective fact that its ministry is not universally accepted by or acceptable to other Christians. The significance of this situation is within the comprehension of any congregation, and it may well furnish a point of contact between the local church and the issues of ecumenical concern. Here is a ministry which, in the doctrine of virtually every church, is established in response to the calling of Christ—for the purpose of ministering *to* Christ's own people the Word and Sacraments by which He is in their midst, and ministering *with* them in their service of making Him known among all men. Yet this ministry that exists solely to represent Christ and to serve Him carries with it a tragic misrepresentation and disservice because there is no form of it that is not questioned as to its validity by large sections of the Church. Thus the redemption we believe to be freely and universally offered by Christ is, when offered by His ministers, subject to all manner of restrictions and contingencies imposed by the limited scope of the ministerial authorization and acceptance. It is not difficult for the members of a local congregation to understand that while this lack of catholicity may not seem to be seriously restrictive of the minister's service to them, it is disastrously crippling to their common service to the Evangel; and that when the Church is disabled in its mission it is, by definition, disabled from being a whole Church.

From this glimpse of the minister's predicament in a disunited Church, the people may turn to see that it is not essentially different from their own. The ministry rendered defective by our divisions is not merely the *minister's* ministry but the *Church's* ministry. From the standpoint of Protestant conviction the harm that is done affects the ministry of every Christian—the mutual ministry of believers to one another, and the universal priesthood of believers in their offering of the Good News of God in Christ to the world. It is this common ministry, to which every Christian is ordained by his baptism, by the act of confessing his faith and accepting the consequent call to be a witness to that faith, that is damaged by our disunity.

That this should be understood and taken to heart by the congregation is a part of the work of bringing ecumenicity into the life of the local church. It is something to be presented and interpreted in preaching, and when this is done the preacher is furthering the participation of his people in the Ecumenical Reformation.

There is a second point of contact between the issue of catholicity, as it is currently under discussion in the Ecumenical Movement, and the interests and responsibilities of the local congregation. And preaching may be the means of bringing the two together.

The problem of catholicity is essentially the problem of the Church's adequacy in presenting and representing the whole Gospel of Christ. It is therefore a question that is much more comprehensive than the question of the Church's order, in the sense of its polity and organization. Catholicity involves the Church's message, its worship, its sacramental life, its ministry, the quality of its fellowship, its relation to other Christians, and its understanding and prosecution of its mission in the world. The question of catholicity leads every church to ask concerning itself: "Is this church such a body, in its form, character, and action, that Christ is recognizably its Head? Is it wholly responsible and responsive to Him in all things?"

From the standpoint of this meaning of catholicity—and it is the fundamental meaning—we must say that no church possesses catholicity; no church is able with fullness and completeness to "show forth" Christ. Yet the conception of catholicity must be for every church the standard by which it judges all its ways. One of the most significant gifts of the Ecumenical Movement is the new willingness —now fortified by a considerable body of experience and technique— to engage in a searching enterprise of self-examination on the basis of ampler standards of catholicity. Indeed we may say that this work of lively self-criticism, in terms of the criteria of catholicity that have become steadily more adequate as a result of the ecumenical encounter and challenge, is at this stage a more significant accomplishment of ecumenicity than any achievements in the realm of church union.

Not only is preaching a means of communicating the meaning of this enterprise; it may also be a way of actually involving a congregation in it existentially. Preaching can aid the local church in applying that method that the Anglo-Catholic spokesmen were right in commending to all churches—the "going behind the rival doctrines to something which they all, in various ways, misrepresent." Until local congregations gain some understanding of this essential ecumenical method, ecumenicity will remain very largely a preoccupation of an ecclesiastical officialdom. The method involves two kinds of function and skill. There is, first, the critical function, especially the self-critical—the acknowledgment that the rival doctrines and practices actually do misrepresent that to which they intend to testify. Second, there is the endeavor of recognition and appreciation —the discernment, after "going behind" all the misrepresentations, of the common faith and common life that could not be misrepresented if they were not in some sense there.

In all this the preacher has a teaching responsibility, and until it is widely and effectively exercised the plea for "ecumenicity at the grass-roots" will remain a pious hope without any program for its realization. He can, for example, help his people see that differences in the manner of expressing a truth do not imply differences in the value ascribed to it or in the measure of devotion accorded it. This seems an elementary point, yet it is given surprisingly little attention in attempts to interpret one denomination to another. It is needed to correct the distorted impression that every denomination conveys when it develops its own apologetic. In giving special emphasis to some doctrine or practice, which they regard as distinctively their own, communions go far beyond the claim of guarding a peculiar treasure for the sake of the whole Church; they repeatedly imply that they are the only Christians who recognize the full worth of this treasure or even care very much about its safety. Listening to spokesmen for Catholicism as they explain how the value of continuity is safeguarded by episcopacy and by liturgical uniformity, one would suppose that other churches have no concern whatever for continuity of Christian faith and life. They need to remind themselves that some of the churches that stress continuity by means of a succession of officers have sometimes been among the most laggard in providing for another kind of continuity—the communication of the faith from one generation to another through effective means of Christian education and evangelism. Hearing some of my own denominational colleagues in their advocacy of the ways of the free churches, one would suppose that no other denomination believes in the freedom of the Christian man or is in any way interested in safeguarding this freedom. Members of other churches, one must infer, are either unaware of the extent to which they have surrendered their liberty, or are actually in love with their chains!

The next major thrust of the ecumenical enterprise cannot occur apart from the development of informed churchmanship—that is to say, an informed laity—that will be increasingly aware of the great common concerns and devotions that are "behind" our varied expressions of them. This does not mean a cavalier dismissal of significant differences between one communion and another. It does mean that we shall all be much less ready than in the past to translate variety of practice into difference of Christian motivation and valuation— that we shall not move so swiftly to the inference that because our brethren of another denomination have a different manner of expressing their allegiance to some aspect of the Christian faith therefore they value it more highly or set less store by it than we do.

In the whole realm of polity, for example, all churches have the problem of establishing a working balance and interplay of values which, in their nature, must be held in tension. Every church—like every form of human society—must find some answer to the problem of freedom and order. Every church must resolve the issue of confessional standards; it must on the one hand provide a sufficiently definite confessional requirement to serve as one of the differentia between itself and secular society (and whether this is called a "creed," or a "confession of faith," or a "covenant" does not alter its basic significance), and on the other hand must give heed to safeguarding the essentially personal character of Christian faith, which confessional requirements must not be allowed to violate. All churches must find ways of bringing into dynamic balance the claims of historic tradition versus the need for spontaneity and innovation;

of faith as "delivered" versus faith as personal immediacy; of the authority of the Word versus the authority of the Spirit; of continuity versus contemporaneity; of the necessity for programs and institutions as means for making faith effective in culture and society versus the right of faith to bring all programs and institutions, including its own, to judgment.

Every denomination has to find some way of resolving these issues. Its polity is its particular answer to these universal problems of the Church. The fact that its solution combines these dynamic ingredients in somewhat different proportions from the formula adopted by another communion is not to be construed as signifying that it values any of them either less or more than does the other denomination.

One form of the mutual recognition that is acknowledged to be a precondition of ecumenical progress is this understanding that the practices of another denomination are attempted solutions—and are real and valid solutions—of the common problems of all the churches, and that the answers embodied in church polity are contingent and relative, not the ultimate issues of Christian faith.

From the vantage point gained by this "going behind" divergent traditions and practices, the members of a congregation may be given a fresh perspective on their own church life, and begin to view it both with new appreciation and new humility. It is universally acknowledged that one of the most valuable gifts of the Ecumenical Movement is the heightened rigor and acuity of self-criticism it encourages. If this gift is to be widely appropriated it must be made available by the preacher. If he has the responsibility for communicating to the congregation the distinctive tradition in which it stands, does he not have also the responsibility for conveying this new power of self-appraisal that is a chief means to that continuing reformation that Protestantism declares to be a mark of the living Church?

In this connection it is worth reflecting that ecumenicity need not be unrelievedly and incorrigibly solemn. Just as Christian faith enables us as individuals to view the contingent and finite aspects of our own life with a measure of humor and gentle irony, so are there resources of ecclesiastical hilarity that ought to be marshalled against the pretensions every denominational apologetic embodies. We need to develop skill in recognizing how many of the traits we find unattractive and the claims we regard as exaggerated in other denominations have their correlatives—or at least their mirror images—in our own.

The healthiest method of illustration is probably in terms of one's own denomination simply because that is the only way an exercise in self-criticism can be honestly conducted. When a Congregationalist is critical of his Catholic brother's susceptibility to the impressiveness of hierarchical rank, he may well reflect upon the propensity of Congregationalists for setting up hierarchies of other sorts. There is the rank of "influential" churches and ministers, which is sometimes as oppressive as any hierarchy of formal status. There is the rank of "princes of the pulpit," that homiletical prelacy that sometimes shows little regard for the dominical standard whereby the "greatest" is the "servant"—in this case the faithful steward of the Word of God. There is the hierarchy of "big wheels" in industry and public affairs—the Protestant monsignors, who are encouraged to throw their weight around in church activities for which their competence is often difficult to detect.

If we are sometimes inclined to be skeptical of what seems to be on the part of Methodists a rather naïve trust in the omnicompetence of organization, we may be encouraged to remember how much organizational effort some of the rest of us expend in maintaining the fiction that we are unorganized. The number of committees, seminars, and commissions we require to keep everything spontaneous and informal is appalling.

If some of the forms and practices of episcopacy seem at times anachronistic, the perpetuation in the ecclesiastical realm of monarchical and aristocratic social systems that are happily outmoded, we need to recall how many of the slogans and battle cries that stir Congregational blood—may it be said?—and secrete Congregational adrenalin are addressed to equally archaic situations. When we speak of our mission to defend freedom of worship, one would suppose we expected just around the corner to meet a James I, announcing that he will make nonconformists "conform themselves, or harrie them out of the land, or else do worse." When we call our own and kindred denominations "free churches" we seem to imagine the imminent likelihood that here in America other churches will be established by law and subsidized by the state.

If we detect in other denominations what strikes us as an undue attachment to tradition, it may lead us to consider how often those of us who call ourselves nontraditional are tyrannized by the lack of it—or by the tradition that we must have no traditions. Some day we shall discover—and it will come to us as a gift of the ecumenical encounter—what a liberating thing it is to leave some matters to governance by judiciously selected traditions, so that we may be free to bring the maximum energy of thought and decision to the real issues that require a fresh attack by the Christian mind.

If we see tendencies to smugness in ecclesiastical and theological orthodoxy—an assumption of knowing the answer to every important question of Christian faith and life—we may do well to meditate on the smugness of dissent—the implied claim that we are exempt from the necessity of even looking for the answers. After all, which is the more regrettable, a theological dogmatism that is overconfident of its possession of the truth, or a theological flippancy that dismisses as irrelevancies the great issues of truth and error that have occupied responsible Christian minds through the centuries?

Some tasks of self-criticism appear to call for a gently satirical approach. If this is so, it is because they involve problems that are, after all, secondary and peripheral. We can afford to deal half-humorously with questions of polity because we cannot afford anything but profound and penitential seriousness when we come to the central and decisive issues, which test not merely our conceptions but our commitments and dedications. What Protestant, having learned the rudiments of ecumenicity, can feel anything but humility in the presence of examples of the devout life that are unmistakable and authentic expressions of Catholic piety? Who of us, as members of "old-line Protestant churches," can entertain any feelings of superiority when we observe the apostolic virility and evangelistic zeal of other Christians whom we have superciliously assigned to "fringe sects"? Evanston said:

We in the World Council are committed to a fellowship in which we are ready to bring our convictions under scrutiny in the presence of our fellow Christians and in the presence of the living Christ. In common we seek to know the judgment of the Word of God upon these convictions as to any error which may be involved in them.[23]

This responsibility for bringing convictions under the judgment of the Word of God and under the scrutiny of the great Church and of its living Lord, is one that cannot be assigned exclusively to church officials and ecumenical enthusiasts; it is a task for the whole Church —that is to say for all the members of the Church. It must be presented to them in manageable form, with understandable clarity, and with compelling urgency. A chief means of doing this is the preaching ministry.

In pursuance of this task we are to remember that our purpose is vastly greater than the furtherance of a movement called "ecumenical." It is more than the challenging of our separate ways through submission to scrutiny by one another; it is a resubmission of ourselves to scrutiny by our one Lord. It is a looking beyond the Church's present life to the objective Source of its faith and message. A pertinent passage from P. T. Forsyth concludes:

. . . The Union of the Churches can never be brought about on a basis of subjective and empirical religion, i.e., of religion which is more full of its experience than of the source which creates the experience, and creates the Church. It can never be brought about just because it is in the air, nor because it seems to meet democratic aspirations. . . .

The divided Churches have become weak, and even futile, through the excessive growth of religious subjectivity. "That must be true which does me good; that must be real which impresses me." Religion indeed is not possible without experience; but we have worn the idea of Christian experience thin. . . . Experience tells me I am saved, but could any experience assure me the whole world will be saved? Such theology does not pierce the depths or grasp the certainty of the divine purpose; it becomes but spiritual psychology. We have no science of God, but only a science of religion. We pursue a theology of consciousness; but we do not explain our state of consciousness by God's treatment of us to begin with. We believe in God's fatherhood by a mere analogy from man's. We postpone revelation to religion; which is an entire inversion. And

that does not make for unity. For we are not one as religious but as redeemed, and especially from petty piety. . . .

Union must be what our faith is—an act less of sympathy than of
obedience to the authority of Love's moral and sovereign Gospel. Experience is one thing, and may be but fraternal; faith is another, and must
be royal. . . . Faith is a matter of experience, but experience is not
faith. And the difference is that in faith we are more concerned with the
object than with the experience. Faith is more than piety. It is more
concerned with the nature of the object than with the mood of the subject. It is more interested in our justification than in our peace.[24]

. . . When we are commissioned to preach we are commanded to do what can never be done by men such as we. Whenever our utterance becomes proclamation of the Word a miracle has happened, the true transubstantiation whereby the human word, indistinguishable as to its accidents from any other word spoken by men, is transformed as to its substance into the authentic, divine Gospel. To preach the Word is beyond the power of sinful men, even though they are justified sinners; the Holy Spirit is the only preacher. Yet though the Church's preaching is not in itself the Word, it presupposes a Word that has been given and bears witness to it. The Church knows that "Christ died for sinners" is a bare formula until the sinner hears it as "Christ died for me." . . . To feed the hungering multitudes she brings her five loaves and two fishes—a veritable foolishness; but this is all she can do, and it is commanded. . . .

But if this is faith's foolishness in the eyes of the world, it is faith's secret wisdom to know that what God has done He can and will do again. For we ourselves received His Word in no other way than this. Perhaps we heard it suddenly, as a man spoke of the forgiving grace of God; perhaps it stole into our minds and hearts so silently that we cannot tell whence it came. But however it came to us, did not God speak His Word through the witness of men like ourselves—preachers or cobblers, learned scribes or unlettered saints—who testified to a crucified and risen Lord! That God should speak to men through our witness seems incredible till we remember that it has been through the witness of other men that God has spoken to us.

H. F. LOVELL COCKS [1]

CHAPTER V

The Communicable Word

INTRODUCING the second volume of the Amsterdam Series, the editor calls attention to one notable feature of the studies that preceded the First Assembly of the World Council of Churches. He observes that for the first time in the modern era a great ecumenical gathering had recognized that the problems of proclaiming the Gospel in the East and the West are fundamentally the same. The distinctions that once differentiated the evangelistic programs and methods of the so-called younger churches from those of the churches in the Western world are out of date. Neither in the East nor in the West is there today a *Corpus Christianum*, a general Christian culture, with which the *Corpus Christi*, the Church, may establish reciprocal and mutually supportive relations. Everywhere in the world the Church confronts once again the characteristic apostolic situation.

Doubtless this thesis can be pressed too far, for there are important differences between the position of the Church in lands where Christianity has been known for many centuries and the countries to which it has come quite recently. In some respects the task of the Church is the more baffling in nations where its presence is generally accepted. T. S. Eliot remarks on the ambiguous position of the Church in the Western world—where, he says, we do not have a Christian society, nor a pagan society, but a *neutral* society, in which the practice of Christianity is tolerated.

I am not concerned with the problems of Christians as a persecuted minority. When the Christian is treated as an enemy of the State, his course is very much harder, but it is simpler. I am concerned with the

dangers to a tolerated minority; and in the modern world it may turn
out that the most intolerable thing is to be tolerated.[2]

Whatever the shadings of difference may be—and they are important—it is clear that the churches both in the East and the West
are in a missionary position; and the recognition of this fact, especially in the West, has enabled them in a new way to begin to learn
from one another.

The "problem of communication," as it is generally called, to
which we turn our attention in this chapter, has of course been with
the Church from the beginning. In modern times, however, it has
usually been regarded as most specifically a problem of the missionary
enterprise. With the close relationship between the International
Missionary Council and the World Council of Churches, with their
continuous collaboration, particularly in considering the task of
evangelism, and now with this recognition of the missionary status
of the Church everywhere, the problem of communication is set in
a wider context, and is being approached with resources of competence and experience that give promise of productive work.

The problem of communication presents itself in three aspects.

First, there is the general problem of language itself—the powers
and the limitations of our linguistic symbols in satisfying the demands
of the realities that are symbolized, the intentions of those who use
them, and the comprehension of those to whom they are expected to
convey meanings.

The second aspect of the problem as it affects the preacher derives
from the fact that much of the traditional—and some of us would
hold, the indispensable—language of Christian speech is unfamiliar
to the men and women of our day. The truth is that it is almost as
strange in the ears of many church members as it is for those outside
the Church. Further, if the words themselves have currency they may
be employed with a meaning very different—sometimes almost opposite—from their significance in a Christian context. We have also
to face the fact that there is less and less likelihood that people will
encounter the language of Christian speech in a Christian context
anywhere outside the Church. The *Saturday Review of Literature*
recently reported the results of a study of the sources of ideas
that reach the people of the United States. It declared that 49

per cent of all ideas now come from the radio and television, 21 per cent from the newspapers, 11 per cent from magazines, 11 per cent from the movies, and only 8 per cent from books.[3] The power of the pulpit, judged by the criteria this study employed, was not investigated. What the inquiry suggests is that the principal arteries of traffic for ideas in this country are through media the Church has scarcely tried to use, or in its attempted use of them has not shown itself notably adept.

The third phase of the problem of communication arises from the fact that the Christian faith is a totality which is ultimately indivisible. Every part of it—its theology, its understanding of faith, its ethic, its doctrine of the Church, its conception and practice of worship—is dependent on every other part. To attempt to describe any aspect of it in isolation from the whole is to attempt what is finally an impossible task. This is true not only of the Christian faith but of other religions as well, as the missionaries have learned. These religions are also unified, self-consistent wholes; they cannot be supplanted piecemeal. It is not possible to substitute Christian ethics for, let us say, Hindu ethics without coming to terms with the theology on which Hindu ethics is based, and without imparting the whole view to which the Christian ethic organically belongs. That "whole view" may be in very simple form, but it is a whole.

Christianity cannot be offered as a living faith simply by listing its constituent elements under the proper headings and subheadings and trying to explain it by comparison with analogous beliefs and practices in some other religion. The devotee of the other religion will recognize, for one thing, that his own faith is being misrepresented as it is broken apart in analysis. And the cataloguing of the elements which, from an intellectual viewpoint, constitute Christianity will equally misrepresent it, so that it will not actually be offered as an alternative *religious faith*. Something beyond these theological, ethical, and cultic ingredients is required, by which the congeries is made a whole. For Christian faith this creative, whole-making act is not logical synthesis or discovery, but revelation. Christian understanding comes ultimately not by the informing or sharpening of the mind, but by the renewing of the mind. How does the Christian preacher or teacher work for this new mind in those who are strangers to the Gospel? How can he communicate what is involved in this renewal, when the very terms of communication he must use belong to a totality that cannot be understood until the renewal has taken place?

To put the problem of communication in a somewhat ruthless way: How are we to speak meaningfully to people concerning a faith that is alien to their own world view, when we must use language which they do not understand, or which, if they do understand it, is an inadequate medium for disclosing the reality it attempts to symbolize?

One further thrust into the problem, and we come to what is in many ways the central dilemma of the preacher in this matter of communication; the issue with which the evangelist must continually grapple. On the one side he knows that nothing less than the whole Gospel, in all its drastic newness and revolutionary power, is sufficient for dealing with our human predicament; only the whole Gospel is really Gospel. On the other side, he knows that the full Gospel comes to men as a scandal and an offense. This has always been so, but perhaps never more acutely so than in our own time; for the Christian faith deals violently, one after another, with the cherished presuppositions by which modern man lives. "The Strange New World Within the Bible," of which Barth speaks, is not only strange and new; it is repellent in its strangeness and novelty. It is not a world in which the final and most decisive truth is one that smart men can think up for themselves. It is not the last term in a finely-wrought logical system. It is not the answer to a sequence of progressively more intelligent questions men have been learning to ask about their existence.

What a scandalous business this Christian proclamation is when viewed from the assumptions of the contemporary world! How it offends and threatens all the secure bases of thought and action! It is rooted in what the theologians call "the scandal of particularity." For the modern mind the most valid truth is abstract and general. But the Christian faith is stubbornly—almost mercilessly—centered in the concrete and the particular.

And what absurd particulars! One Book, the Bible—this, amid all the world's vast literature, uniquely confronting us with the Word of God. One people, one nation, one succession of events—limited in space and time, occurring far out on the periphery of secular history, yet the chosen medium for disclosing God's will and way with a fulness not approached elsewhere in all the world's story. One atoning act—of which we must say that while men are never without evidence of God's mercy, they know it to be the mercy of God the Father and Redeemer only in this act—and in this event alone He offers His very self in all His redemptive grace and love. One community of redemption, the Church—miserable in its weakness, its sinfulness, and its apostasy, yet the organ of Christ's activity in the world: His Body. These things are scandalous.

Here the issue is sharp and clear. Either we break with the Christian faith and go over to some form of the Hegelian rejection of particularity, or we have to come to terms with the scandalous particularity of the Gospel.

There is the scandal of the Gospel's attack upon our autonomy and self-sufficiency. It is offensive to be reminded that we are creatures and not creators, and that the meaning of life is to be found in a freedom that is ultimately obedience. It is outrageous to be told that our life is not our own to do with as we please—that it was purchased for us and it is owed.

There is the twofold scandal of forgiveness: first the shattering acknowledgment that we need to be forgiven; second, the incredible truth that we can be forgiven—that forgiveness is possible in the radical sense in which the Gospel offers it: forgiveness not only for what we have done and left undone but for what we are.

There is the scandal of a reconciliation with God—a justification that is free because no one can earn it. Surely our goodness must count for something! Surely our hard-won moral achievements must impress God just a little bit!

It is impossible to present the Gospel without this offense. Although it is true that the Gospel cannot be ultimately alien to man and his needs, it is alien to the "old man"; it is alien until man has been driven to face the central problem of his existence. In its study of "The Christian Witness in a Revolutionary World" the International Missionary Council said: "Christian faith identifies itself with men's needs, but never with their desires. Christian faith identifies itself with men's questions, but never with their answers."

D. T. Niles, in an address on evangelism given at the Evanston meeting of the World Council, said:

> Surely we are faced with a basic contradiction between the command to succeed and the need to be faithful to the message with which we are entrusted. The truth is that many who are invited will not come, and that the Master will not send His invitation back to them in a more acceptable form.[4]

Kierkegaard has an entry in his *Journals* in which he comments on the effort to present Christian faith painlessly:

> According to the New Testament, Christianity is the deepest wound that can be inflicted upon a man—and now the modern clergyman is trained in the art of introducing Christianity in such a way that it signifies nothing, and when he is perfect in that he is a paragon. . . . Oh, it is all very well for a barber to become skillful enough to shave off a man's beard without his noticing it; but when it comes to a matter which is expressly intended to wound, the acquisition of such skill in applying it so that it will not be noticed—that is revolting.[5]

The minister enters his pulpit with the foreknowledge that Christian preaching, if done faithfully, will have this offensive, outrageous quality. No trick of evangelistic technique, no discovery of the science of communication, will enable us to by-pass this dilemma. The only ultimately effective agency in proclamation, apart from the miraculous work of the Holy Spirit Himself, is the power to convince and convict and persuade and possess that inheres in the *truth* that is in our Lord Jesus Christ. And this truth does its work radically, smashing man's security and shattering his self-esteem and self-reliance.

One of the Amsterdam papers summarizes the problem very well:

> It is obvious that the task of evangelism has its perils. The Church, by loyal faithfulness to what it has received, may make its message meaningless. [On the other hand] by excessive concern for the contemporary relevance of its utterance, it may be betrayed into unfaithfulness to the Gospel of God's judgment and God's mercy. . . . The problem of evangelism is just the perpetual rediscovery of the narrow way on which alone the Church can be true to its two-fold vocation of faithfulness to God and service to His creatures.[6]

As the subject of communication in the general sense involves intricate questions of philosophy and psychology, so the subject of Christian communication leads inevitably to difficult theological problems. There is the problem of "natural theology." There is the problem of the so-called "point of contact." There is the problem that has been hotly debated in missionary groups as to how far and in what way other religions may be considered as "preparation" for the Gospel. It needs to be urged that this question is equally pertinent to the work of the older churches. How far and in what way can the secular faiths—and antifaiths—that are the religions to which multitudes of our contemporaries and a great many church people give their real allegiance—to what extent may these be regarded as "preparation" for the Gospel?

Obviously, much preaching does not take seriously the problem of communication. The literalist, the "fundamentalist," is not even aware of it. He delivers his supply of verbal stereotypes and leaves it, as he would say, to the Holy Spirit to do the rest. But we are not minimizing the work of the Holy Spirit when we question this method. In this regard we observe something of the feeling that is engendered by the repeated invocations of the Holy Spirit in the reports of ecumenical discussions. They are always saying: "On this issue, and that, we are agreed; but as regards these others we must await the further leading of the Holy Spirit to bring us into unity." That statement may be a humble confession of human perplexity and of the need for illumination. If it is repeated too often, however, it may become simply a pious formula for defending our immobility and our refusal to be changed as we must be changed. Our need of leading by the Holy Spirit is evident enough; but there is sometimes need of more evidence that we are *willing to be led*. The fundamentalist's cavalier dismissal of the problem of communication seems to me to raise a similar issue. We do not question that only the Holy Spirit can make possible speaking "from faith to faith"—that only the Holy Spirit can perform that act of quickening faith by which message becomes Gospel. But does that relieve the preacher from the responsibility of trying to speak an articulate and communicable word? Surely there is some way of being *used* by the Holy Spirit without *tempting* the Holy Spirit.

There is also a good deal of "liberal" preaching that does not take seriously the problem of communication. It does not consider that there is any problem here, because it assumes that if preaching establishes a mood of general religiousness, or ethical tension, or vague reassurance, communication has taken place. The test is whether people are *interested* (a criterion, by the way, for which something can be said), whether they are *"convinced"*—in the sense of agreeing to what has been said, or whether they receive something called *"inspiration"*—which is extremely difficult to define, except that it is supposed to make people feel better. The lack of seriousness here takes the form of an excessive interest in communication merely as a process, and not enough interest in what, Christianly speaking, is being communicated. The "liberal" is disinclined—in part, no doubt, because of his trust in reason and reasonableness—to admit the fundamental insecurity that attends and surrounds all Christian communication, and the enormity of the offense it sometimes provokes. We liberals—and all of us on whom the Divinity School of Yale University has wrought its blessed will are that, whether of the chastened or unchastened variety—continue to want conditions and results in the work of communication for which there is neither precedent nor promise in the calling of the Gospel ministry. As a contemporary treatise on evangelism—the work, significantly, of a Yale Divinity School professor—sharply characterizes our expectations:

What we want is something solid upon which to build, perhaps something like an interest or, even better, a captive audience. We need also the sense of having a product sure to go over, once the right angle of approach to the market is figured. We would like a program for which calculable returns are available, to submit to the people who prefer to invest in sure things rather than in risks. Finally, we could use a sound guarantee so that even the people who won't buy will still be friendly and will still find us good Christian people irresistibly lovable.

None of these things is assured the evangelical church.[7]

If the fundamentalist and the liberal do not take seriously the problem of communication, there is some evidence that others who are more sophisticated and rigorously critical in their analysis of the problem do not take with sufficient seriousness the *obligation* of communication. From a certain standpoint this seems to me to be true of Karl Barth. Those who recognize the fundamental and invaluable work Barth has done and is still doing in his study of the nature of the "church proclamation," need also to realize that he has not completed the task and that much further work has yet to be done. One expresses this judgment with a good deal of hesitancy. Someone has said that Barth has given us some of the most skillful and penetrating theological argument of modern times—all to prove that there is nothing in theology. Similarly, one might say that Barth has labored with a passion and dedication exhibited by few other thinkers of our day in an effort to communicate something he insists is incommunicable. It is interesting, however, that as uncompromising as he often seems to be he has made concessions in the interest of communication. He says he has given up the use of the expression "wholly other," because it was misunderstood. He says that what was described as "the theology of crisis" is "now behind." "It could not," says Barth, "and ought not to last longer than a moment." [8] But it is probably fair to say that Barth and "neo-orthodoxy" (if there is any such thing) have not taken the obligation—and, prior to this, the possibility—of communication as seriously as we could wish.

We preachers must take it seriously; we must take it as seriously as the Ecumenical Movement, and that is very seriously indeed. The work now being done in this field, under ecumenical auspices, has the sharpest relevance for the preaching ministry. It brings us, with a thud of bodily contact, up against the central concerns of our vocation—what preaching is, and especially its *milieu*: the real "content," so to speak, of the modern mind and spirit to which it is addressed. It is in this field that the basic work in homiletics is being done. And we ought to follow it with the absorption and sense of excitement it deserves.

One might be timid about suggesting this if it were a subject so abstruse and inaccessible that a busy preacher would need a sabbatical year in a seminary library to make any approach to it. But it is not. Much can be done in the time some of us give to the books and magazines on pulpit manners—how to hold the homiletical teacup with the little finger properly curved. We could especially save some time from tomes containing 465 "illustrations for preachers"—books which have helped sermonic communication about the way sun spots help radio.

This business of communication is our business; it is much more our business than the work of "making sermons." It has become a major subject of ecumenical inquiry; but it is also an ecumenical concern that must be brought out of the commissions and formal study groups into the attention of parish ministers who are carrying the responsibility continuously and in face-to-face relationship with ordinary men and women—the men and women who *don't* read books and *do* get 49 per cent of their ideas from radio and television. The theoreticians can help to state the problem, but the answers will be found by those who are actually carrying on the evangelistic task of the Church. There is a great need for groups of ministers in local communities who will take the pains to get a general knowledge of the problem as it is now being stated and restated for us, and then undertake actual experiments to be subjected to mutual criticism.

There is need of tackling this problem in its relation to the Church's employment of radio and television. Protestant bodies continue to spend hundreds of thousands of dollars, and to use millions of dollars' worth of broadcast time provided by the industry on a public service basis, without asking the fundamental questions about the limitations and possibilities of these media in the service of the Gospel. In the Church's use of radio and television there has been some improvement of technique. Nearly everyone now knows that broadcasting does not address "a vast audience of millions," but many audiences of one or two or three, and that it is a mistake to talk to a woman in her living room as if she were in a public meeting—or even as if she were sitting in a pew in church. But we have scarcely looked beyond these elementary considerations.

Is preaching really possible via radio and television? Can preaching be done outside the context of the Church? Can this context of the Church's worship and fellowship be constructed by remote control? Can broadcasting be considered as an instrument of evangelism— that is, is it evangelistically effectual in any direct way? Some of us have often wondered about the floods of letters and contributions radio evangelists are said to receive. Do they come from persons who have themselves been converted, or who know anyone who has been converted by radio or television? Or do they come from persons who imagine—perhaps because of the evangelist's reference to "hundreds of letters"—that somebody is being converted? This is not to impugn the evangelists' motives, but to ask the kind of question that a responsible Church must begin to ask. Can broadcasting ever be more than preparatory to a hearing of the Gospel, and what is the nature of this preparation? May there not be a solid basis for believing that the form of this preparation is narrative and dramatic—so that while broadcasting cannot be used to preach the Gospel directly it can tell the story of man's life in such a way that it demands the answer of the Gospel. But can that answer be given except by the Gospel in the fellowship of the Church? There is need of a more fundamental inquiry into these problems than has yet been pursued. It ought to be undertaken by those who are actually making use of these media.*

This problem of communication is one we dare not evade. To be indifferent about it on alleged theological grounds is to detach theology from the Evangel. To preach—as some fundamentalists do—of the Incarnation in words that are wholly discarnate from the viewpoint of the hearers, and of the Atonement without making an effort to be "at one" with men's understanding and needs, and of God's infinite condescension from a standpoint of dogmatic arrogance and self-sufficiency—is to unpreach the Gospel in the act of preaching.

The materials that are helpful in stating the problem and in stimulating experiment and reflection are readily accessible. There is Hendrik Kraemer's book—now almost a classic—*The Christian Message in a Non-Christian World*. Despite an extreme viewpoint on some matters it is indispensable, for it has become a kind of universal point of reference in the discussion of this problem. For a balanced consideration of Kraemer one might suggest a brief essay by Walter Horton, entitled *Between Hocking and Kraemer*, in Volume One of the reports from the Madras Conference. There is the second volume of the Amsterdam Series, *The Church's Witness to God's Design*, dealing with the subject of evangelism—particularly that

---

* A promising start has been made in the Communications Research Project, begun in 1952 under the auspices of the Broadcasting and Film Commission of the National Council of Churches, in co-operation with the Divinity School of Yale University.

brief and jolting section setting forth the "Axioms of the Modern Man." There is a pamphlet issued by the Study Department of the World Council, called *Evangelization of Modern Man in Mass Society*, and perhaps the report of the Whitby Conference of the International Missionary Council, published under the title *Renewal and Advance*. From there on a man is competent to be his own guide.

This may very well be the conclusion of this chapter. It has attempted to suggest the nature of the problem and to intimate something of its urgency. If what has been written thus far should prompt anyone to investigate the resources available from the Ecumenical Movement in this field—especially if any small group should be encouraged to work at it experimentally and self-critically—this statement will have achieved one of its chief objectives.

The remaining comments are in the nature of footnotes—brief observations on two or three aspects of this interest.

First, on the language of Christian speech. Those of us who welcome the return of theological seriousness, and who believe that there is an indispensable vocabulary of distinctively Christian terms for which there are no substitutes, need to guard against making this conviction an excuse for obscurity. We are not permitted to join that literary cult which regards plain talk as a form of philistinism. In a paper read by a brother-minister on the occasion of his installation in a parish, he says: "It is possible to hypothecate the perpetuation of sense-perceptive area-trends beyond the area of sense perception." As he was engaged in stating his faith, and this great affirmation comes after some reference to the Holy Catholic Church and the Forgiveness of Sins, we surmise he was trying to say something about belief in Eternal Life. Now it would be interesting to know whether he believes in the life everlasting; but when it comes to knowing whether he believes in the perpetuation of sense-perceptive area-trends beyond the area of sense-perception, our indifference is positively monumental. And so is that of his people, who were there to hear what he thought about the Christian faith.

Huge Vernon White of the Pacific School of Religion once made an informal statement to a group of ministers, in which he distinguished between "theological language" and "Christian language." Theological language, as he viewed it, is technical language trained specialists use in their discourse in the interest of condensation and precision. It is not the language of preaching. There is, however, a *Christian* language that is indispensable for defining the ideas in which the meaning of the Christian faith is articulated—ideas that are *not faith* but that are necessary for interpreting the faith to the understanding. This is language not merely of intellectual conversation but of liturgy and devotion. It is characteristically the language of the Bible. Some of the words in this Christian language are irreplaceable, because there are no substitutes for them. There is no exact synonymn for the word "sin"; try to find one that does not blunt its incisive character. There is no substitute for the word "grace"—not "goodness," not even "love." And there are many others.

This has never been said more trenchantly than by P. T. Forsyth in his Lyman Beecher lectures:

To discard that [distinctively Christian] language entirely is to maim the utterance of the Gospel. To substitute a vocabulary of mere humane sympathies or notions for the great phrases and thoughts which are theology compressed into diamonds is like the attempt to improve a great historic language, which is a nation's record, treasure and trust, by reducing it to Saxon monosyllables, and these to phonetics. I cannot conceive a Christianity to hold the future without words like grace, sin, judgment, repentance, incarnation, atonement, redemption, justification, sacrifice, faith and eternal life. No words of less volume than these can do justice to the meaning of God, however easy their access to the minds of modern men. It needs such words to act on the scale of God and of the race. And the preacher who sets out to discard them or, what is more common, to eviscerate them, is imperilling the great Church for a passing effect with the small.[9]

This means that we face the task of reconstituting a genuinely Christian language—certainly in the life of the Church. It is not easy, for the problem is not merely one of disuse but of corruption. What, for example, can the man in the street think when he hears the minister address a prayer to "Gracious Lord," and then finds, as I did the other day, that in a single issue of a slick magazine the requirements of "gracious" living include the following items: a four-thousand dollar automobile, a room covered with carpet at thirty-five dollars a yard, and a supply of twelve-year-old Scotch whiskey?

If the Church is to know what it is and what it believes, we must learn to speak the language of our faith. The young ministers working in the East Harlem Protestant Parish in New York City have, in one particular at least, short-cut the problem by returning to the Greek. It is rather moving to hear Puerto Ricans, some of them unable to read or write, speak of inviting fellow-members of the Church to share in an "agape meal."

Doubtless many scriptural figures of speech, with their Oriental and pastoral setting, have little meaning for contemporary hearers. But we need to be careful lest our modern substitutes become evasions and actually parry the thrust of the biblical word. It may be a sign of over-scrupulosity, but I squirmed a good deal the other day when I attended a funeral service and heard the officiating minister tamper with Revelation. He was reading the passage: "These are they which came out of great tribulation and have washed their robes and made them white"—and here his heart quailed, and he wound up, "and made them white in the Spirit of Christ." Doubtless the phrase "the blood of the Lamb" presents very great difficulties. But many of us do not believe that we are brought through the really great tribulation—the ultimate tribulation—by the Spirit of Christ, but by a deed actually done for us—on a hill and by the opening of a tomb.

One of the books produced by the Study Department of the World Council makes this point incisively.

. . . The Church must understand, come to terms with, and perpetuate the Biblical language and vocabulary as a living factor in its life, liturgy, and preaching. *The most important single function of dogmatic theology is the preservation and exposition of the Biblical language as a fitting vehicle for the Gospel as proclaimed by the Church to this day.* Unless theology is able to do this, the Church will be separated from the Biblical source of its continued enlightenment.[10]

This question of language in our day is more than a matter of enabling Christians to converse concerning their faith. Denis de Rougemont has pointed out how much of our international and cultural confusion is due to the lack of any common language—so that such words as *liberty, authority, justice, democracy, truth* not only have many meanings but may even have opposite meanings. He believes that the nearest approach to a common language—one that is supranational and supracultural—is to be found in the liturgical language of the Church. The Anglican who attends a Lutheran service, or even the Reformed churchman who attends a Roman Mass, finds, if he knows the Christian language at all, that what he hears is familiar. De Rougemont believes that one way in which Christian people will come to know their membership of one another is to discover how much this language *is* a common language, with a common meaning, in the midst of the confusions and contradictions of words in the world outside. And one of the supreme tasks of the Church is to restore to humanity a common and meaningful speech. De Rougemont writes:

> The true problem of the century is that of the community. It is bound up with the problem of a common language. Liturgy can contribute toward recreating and authenticating this language; but only under two equally determinative conditions: it must remain Biblical at its source, and it must find a contemporaneous form.[11]

Not only through liturgy but through preaching as well, this common language, Biblical at its source, but contemporaneous in form, may be put again on men's lips.

It is said that in the days of the Arian controversy, theology was vigorously discussed in the barbershops of Italy. Though there are no reports of a resurgence of theological interest in our own time in precisely that quarter, it is far from impossible that theology in the best sense should become a subject of lively interest and conversation among Christian people. And we need to recognize how much human discourse is always on the verge of becoming theological. Doubtless most young ministers going to their first parishes are shocked, as were some of us ministers of an earlier generation, to discover how well people are able to control their enthusiasm when they pass along items of biblical and theological information they have labored mightily to acquire. It is easy to put this down as a fundamental lack of religious seriousness. And yet, as we learn really to listen to the speech of our fellows, and set less store by the terms of our professional vocabulary, we begin to hear—underneath many little questionings, and behind the many brave assertions—the real question, de profundis, the question about God. And because that question is incoherently there, it can be helped to more articulate expression. Whatever our success, or want of it, in encouraging theological conversation in secular circles, it is not beyond reasonable hope that there may be a recovery of a Christian manner of speech within the Christian community—without which that community cannot live its full common life, nor genuinely know what it has to communicate to the world.

A second footnote, which will be brief.

We preachers will do well to consider seriously whether the communicable Word may not be essentially the *narrative* Word—not in heaven's name, the anecdotal word, but the *narrative*. What we have to tell is, after all, a story. It is a story of events—of things done and being done, and we make it into an essay—what the magazine editors call a "think piece." It is God's story, and it is also man's story, in the most intimate and personal way.

Undoubtedly the offense in Protestant preaching—and it is not the offense of the Gospel—is its moralism. It is this too simple and unsympathetic moving from the biblical Word (or more likely from some "general principle" of ethics, which we have superimposed on the Bible) into the ethical complexities of man's actual life, and delivering a message of accusation. It is the reduction of a Gospel of deliverance and victory to a carping, life-denying puritanicalism.

The great regulative force that can prevent this distortion is the story itself—especially if we tell it remembering that the Church first came to the world telling the story of the Resurrection.

Theology in its essence is reflection on the sacred story. In the introduction to her series of radio plays on the life of Christ, entitled *The Man Born to Be King*, Dorothy Sayers speaks of the dependence of Christian drama on theology and the dependence of theology on drama.

From the purely dramatic point of view theology is enormously advantageous, because it locks the whole structure into a massive intellectual coherence. It is scarcely possible to build up anything lopsided,

trivial, or unsound on that steely and gigantic framework. Always provided, of course, that two conditions are observed. It must be a *complete*
theology; never was there a truer word than that "except a man believe
rightly he cannot"—at any rate, his artistic structure cannot possibly—
"be saved." A loose and sentimental theology begets loose and sentimental art forms; . . . an ill-balanced theology issues in false emphasis
and absurdity. Conversely, there is no more searching test of a theology
than to submit it to dramatic handling; nothing so glaringly exposes in-
consistencies in a character, a story, or a philosophy as to put it upon the
stage and allow it to speak for itself. Any theology that will stand the
rigorous pulling and hauling of the dramatist is pretty tough in its
texture. Having subjected Catholic theology [and of course she does not
mean Roman Catholic] to this treatment, I can testify that it is very
tough indeed.

Miss Sayers is right. In Christian preaching we speak of events;
and if it can have in it this eventful, dramatic, deedful quality it will
serve the communicable word.

It is to be hoped that someone competent to do so will explore for
us the similarity between this recognition of the essentially *narrative*
character of the Christian message and the *dialectical* method we
associate with Karl Barth. The resemblance seems to be very close.
Starting with the assertion that it is impossible to speak *directly* concerning God—that, as Barth puts it, we do not say "God" merely by
shouting "man" in a loud voice—we are driven to face the fact that
there is no straight-line communication of the Gospel in preaching.
When the truth of God is proclaimed it is only because He Himself
has spoken—as it were, between the humanly spoken sentences—
only because He has broken through the interstices between our
words. There is no direct speech about God; it is in the tension and
ceaseless movement—between despair and hope, between judgment
and mercy, between man's "No" and his "Yes" to the ultimate question of his existence—that the living Word is declared. Just as the
incarnate Word was sent to men *incognito*, disguised in human flesh,
so the reiteration of that Word is always *incognito*. Only when God
Himself acts to quicken faith does the word-in-disguise become
revelation.

This viewpoint comes to climactic expression when Barth, after flinging his thunderous "No" at every hope that man, as man, can learn to speak the Word of God, adds this sentence:

Yet it may be that the Word, the Word of God, which we ourselves shall never speak, has put on our weakness and unprofitableness so that our word, in its very weakness and unprofitableness, has become capable at least of being the mortal frame, the earthen vessel, of the Word of God.[12]

But the form of that incognito, one would add, is a story—the whole salvation history. And it is as this story that we must somehow learn to tell it if the words are to be used as media of communication.

Third, something ought to be said about the obligation of the Christian communicator to be at home in the thought-world of his time. There is an apologetic task that cannot be shirked. We preachers cannot close our eyes to the polemical situation in which the Church makes its testimony today. In few places in the world, if in any, is the evangelistic responsibility one of commending the Christian faith to persons who are religiously neutral—for whom the decision is between the Christian faith and no faith. We have learned in the most tragic and dreadful ways that what Emil Brunner calls "the dimension of the absolute" in men's spirits does not remain unoccupied, and that there are other candidates for occupancy besides the Christian faith. The Church confronts alternative faiths and antifaiths, which claim to offer an interpretation of the meaning and destiny of human existence and which are vigorously contending for the allegiance of men. And their claim to the right to supersede the Christian faith is made partly on grounds that this faith is historically irrelevant and philosophically naïve.

There is much debate around the question as to the propriety of a Christian apologetic, and ecumenical gatherings have debated this issue with some heat. But I think one can say this much at least, with assurance of rather wide agreement: though there is no evading the scandal of the Gospel—which includes a genuine intellectual scandal —nevertheless in the present polemical situation we have to be able to show by apologetic methods where the scandal does not lie. It is not in Jonah and the whale, nor in a literalistic use of the Bible, nor in the rejection of reason within reason's proper sphere. These needless offenses can be cleared away by an apt and adroit apologetic, so that modern man can at least see where the real offense resides. It is not an offense to his reason, but to his autonomy.

When we speak of communication very much ought to be said—and we shall turn to this in our final chapter—concerning the interdependence of the preached word and the word that is spoken wordlessly in the fellowship of the Church and in the action of that fellowship as it gives itself in mercy and love to the world. Whenever missionary groups discuss the question of the so-called "point of contact" between the Christian faith and other religions, they come eventually to the acknowledgment that the real point of contact is the missionary himself. For in him the word becomes living in a way that can never eliminate the need of telling the "story"—the story we can never really incarnate—but that tells some portion of it in the communicable language of compassion and charity.

Finally, no study or solution of the problem of communication can make preaching other than an act of faith. That our words should ever be the means by which God's Word is spoken—the Word that alone can awaken faith and be its answer—is not a consequence of communication but of intervention. Preaching is always in the most radical sense from faith to faith.

Our concluding word may well be a return to the reminder from Lovell Cocks with which we began: that "communication" in its profound Christian meaning—the transubstantiation of our words to become the Word—is always a miracle. That we cannot *compel* or even *initiate* its happening is the humble confession with which all preaching begins. That it *does* happen is our refreshment in the midst of the labor and travail of our calling, and our awe-filled joy before the holy mystery of its occurring.

If the Gospel of the Cross is to be proclaimed in such a fashion that it meets the felt needs of men it must be set forth by a community of men whose own disorder has been effectively dealt with at the Cross. A Church content to remain disunited has no gospel for a disunited world, no gospel, that is, which men, whose fundamental preoccupation is their state of disintegration, can understand. Just in proportion as the Church is becoming growingly discontented with her disunity can she at this moment be trusted with the gospel at all. In this divine discontent, in which her repentance is bringing her to that boundary situation where she really comes to the end of herself and her pride and her complacency, God can use her to help men to see that she is really concerned about the whole of life, about wholeness, about the atonement. Only so can she reveal God.

MAX WARREN [1]

CHAPTER VI

Preaching the Reformation

FROM the vantage point of the Ecumenical Movement we have been looking at some of the deep-running and momentous changes now taking place in the churches. These changes, we have contended, are sufficiently profound and sweeping, and the reorientation of the Church's life that is occurring is sufficiently radical to justify the term "Reformation." Since the sixteenth century there have been numerous revivals and awakenings that influenced wide areas of church life. The most important was one not generally characterized in these terms: it was the extraordinary epoch of missionary endeavor and accomplishment that began about a century and a half ago and that today is far from having spent its force. This modern missionary outthrust of the Church displayed authentic insignia of a reformation. It was generated by a new understanding of the Gospel and of the requirements of obedience to the Gospel; and as men and women obeyed, their understanding of the Gospel's meaning was further deepened and amplified. As one summary puts it:

The missionary movement of the nineteenth century is an overwhelming demonstration of the truth that when Christians act unreservedly upon some part of their calling which they do see, God can release into life all manner of fulfillments of their calling which they did not see.[2]

The Ecumenical Reformation has this in common with other revivals and awakenings: it is not only a summons to recognize the claim of the Gospel and act on the command of the Gospel; it is also a most searching attempt to penetrate the meaning of the Gospel in its interior depths.

What distinguishes the Ecumenical Movement from other post-sixteenth century reformations is the fact that in it the Church is involved *as the Church* in a way that was not true of revival periods or the era of missionary expansion. We have come to see the Church as related to the Gospel in a far more organic and necessary relationship than that of being a means of winning individuals to Christ. Undoubtedly this change has been in part a response to the terrible disciplines of history. As human societies, one after another, have collapsed, we have had to consider afresh the meaning of the Christian society. We have had to think of its relation to these dying orders—and to the new orders that are being born. In many parts of the world, to be able to declare the independence and sovereignty of the Gospel, the Church has had to concern itself consciously with the task of extricating the Christian society from involvement with secular orders now in process of dissolution. We have been learning that history is quite as much discontinuity as continuity, and we have had to ask in a new way whether the Church can rely on history —for example, the kind of history embodied in an historic succession —as the guarantor of its continuing life. With the disappearance of whole peoples—by the tragedies of political change, or, perhaps more terribly, by submersion in the depersonalized mass—Christians have been led to ask what it means to be a *people*. In a day when events have jolted us out of the illusions of a purely evolutionary view of history, out of a cozy historical gradualism into an environment where we are recovering the capacity to think eschatologically, we are having to ask what it means to be an eschatological people, a people of the new age, which the Church was at its beginning.[3]

These are some of the subsurface movements of reformation. The fact that these movements exist—that what comes into public view as the most conspicuous form of change, and the one by which a particular period of reformation is identified, is only one aspect of an inclusive renovation—is another evidence of the radical character of the revolution in which the Church is now involved. Outwardly and publicly, the most conspicuous manifestation of the New Reformation is the struggle of the Church to understand and express its true unity. It is this fact that gives the Ecumenical Reformation its name.

We have now to ask: To what extent and in what forms is the

Ecumenical Reformation itself a subject of preaching? We have considered some of the ways in which it is providing new resources for the preacher—by its recovery of the Bible as we reappropriate the wholeness and unity of Scripture; by its validation of a high conception of the Church; by the accumulation of a growing body of understanding and experiment applicable to the task of Christian communication and evangelism; by the vision of the fullness of the Church's life and message granted to us as we look beyond the disfigurements caused by our separation; and especially by a new and personal seriousness awakened by the knowledge that the Church is dependent, not merely for its hope of unity but for its very existence, on a new act of bringing itself under the Word, an act of submission and resubmission of its whole life and order to the authority of the Word of God. These are some of the gifts mediated to us ministers through the Ecumenical Reformation.

But is this reformation in any sense a subject and intention of the preacher's message? Are we now called purposefully to "preach a reformation"? I believe we are. As the proclaiming of the Gospel is one of the "constitutive" acts of the Church—an act necessary to its being the Church—so is preaching, one may say, a "reconstitutive" act. By the preached Word the Church is formed—not alone by this, but by this necessarily. And by the preached Word the Church is to be reformed. Whether or not we think of the Church as being a "gathered" community in the somewhat technical ecclesiological meaning of that term, there is a sense in which the Church must continually be regathered. To be a living Church it must continually be brought under the crisis and decision of faith. The confronting of the Church with this crisis of the Word is the office of the preacher. And the Church will not be reconstituted, regathered in its wholeness and unity, without the preaching of this reformation.

What is the nature and content of this preaching?

It will not take the form of a rash of sermons on church unity or church union. Certainly no minister who has seen the vision of a Church made new—one of the signs of its renovation being the healing of its divisions—can keep from his preaching the note of yearning for its realization nor cease to offer in prayer and testimony the Church's penitence that this is not yet. But one would preach on the specific subject of church union perhaps about as often as one would describe the organization and program of a mission board of one's denomination. That comparison, indeed, may be fairly apt. That the Church has a mission ought to be a steadily recurrent theme of preaching; but this is different from preaching "about missions" or about the organizational functioning and accomplishments of a denominational mission board. That Christ is one, and His people are one, and that they are called to acknowledge, recognize, and love one another and be visibly one, should be necessary elements in all interpretation of the nature and vocation of the Christian Church. But this is not the same as preaching sermons on church union.

A more cogent distinction can be drawn by looking again to the sixteenth century and setting the preaching of the *Reformation* in contrast with the preaching of the *reformers*. The issues of the Reformation, in the narrower sense—as a specific movement in church history—were not the main burden of the reformers' preaching. These technical problems, doctrinal and ecclesiastical, were discussed in diets and councils, in polemical writings and debates, and—because they had extensive political implications—in high councils of state. But the Reformation as a subject—in the sense of "Let us now have a Reformation of the Church"—was not the topic to which the reformers characteristically addressed themselves in their preaching. They preached the authority of the Bible, the call to repentance, the wonder of salvation by grace, the restored freedom of the Christian man, and the presence and lordship of the risen and living Christ in His Church.

Yet, though there was little preaching of "the Reformation," it was none the less made articulate and real in the preaching of the reformers. People were aware of and participants in a springtide of faith and a rebirth of the Church.

Unless the Ecumenical Reformation is articulated in the Church's preaching it must be a reformation of a very restricted sort—one that is scarcely more than incipient. It will not reach beyond the leaders of interchurch activity, a select company of theologians and biblical scholars, and a small coterie of ecumenical enthusiasts. Indeed, one of the most reliable tests of its vitality is in all likelihood the degree to which it becomes an essential and compelling theme of ordinary, week-by-week preaching in the local church. At the Edinburgh Conference a spokesman for the Youth Group reminded the assembly that the most important forms of ecumenical activity are not the great international and interdenominational meetings. "A real striving for ecumenicity," he insisted, "can and must be undertaken at the heart of each individual confession or church." [4] More recently an officer of the World Council of Churches has said:

[True ecumenicity is] something that happens in the souls of Christians. It is a new understanding of the Body of Christ. If that is true, it concerns . . . the local minister and the ordinary congregation not less but more than it concerns anybody else. The real centre and foundation of ecumenicity lies in the places where, day by day and year by year, souls are fed by Word and Sacrament. [5]

This involvement of the local minister and congregation obviously means something more than the spread of information concerning discussions, issues, and events associated with the work of such organizations as the World Council of Churches. It is more than awareness of developments in what is sometimes called "the ecumenical world"—though some familiarity with these things is in our day a requirement of elementary Christian literacy. The Ecumenical Movement, however, is wider and more comprehensive, and at the same time more local and immediate, than its organizational expressions. Its greatest significance for the local church is not in turning the attention of the congregation toward something external to their basic concerns as members of that church.

The primary way in which the Ecumenical Movement should be influencing the particular church is through its effect upon the way in which the church lives its own life, upon its reading and hearing of the Word of God and its celebration of the Sacraments, and upon the prayers and hymns and the common life which gather round these. [6]

To the demand, which has become almost obsessive in the literature of the Movement, that ecumenicity must become a concern of the local congregation and the "ordinary church member," that it must take the form of "ecumenicity at the grass roots," the service of preaching is assuredly a part of the answer. For the preacher is com-

missioned for the responsibility of acquainting the people of God
with their own story—the story of their ancient pilgrimages and their
present goings forth. The account of the Ecumenical Movement is a
major motif in that story.

If ecumenicity is "something that happens in the souls of Christians," what then are the forms of its happening that may be articulated, interpreted, and furthered in preaching?

*First, preaching is essentially a telling of the mighty acts of God.
The Ecumenical Reformation is evidence of new and mighty acts
being done by Him in our own time. In this sense it is to be preached.*

Like the appearance of the Church at the beginning, the struggle
for the Church's unity is not understandable on the basis of human
impulse and purpose: it is in deepest truth a struggle. Those who are
most profoundly involved in it are continually aware not only that
they are contending with one another, but that there is One who is
contending with them. The natural predilections brought to this
struggle do not lead in the direction of greater unity; the atmosphere
of every serious ecumenical discussion is electric with tension and
volcanic with vast disturbings of men's spirits. "We do not like each
other very much," said the Archbishop of Canterbury at Amsterdam,
"but we are very much alike." Persistence in this task is not due to
any hearty affability, or even to a fundamental personal rapport that
Christians instinctively feel and express when they come together;
the natural effect of this meeting is rather to increase the distance
between them. They find their strongest convictions and deepest
loyalties exposed to questioning and challenge. Moreover, these convictions and loyalties are not merely private concerns, for the participants are always conscious of their representative capacity and their
responsibility for dealing faithfully with the church bodies for which
they try to speak.

It has often been remarked that the first result of the ecumenical
encounter is to arouse in the participants a sharpened sense of the
distinctiveness of their separate ways and to make them more
vigorous in interpreting and defending their own traditions. The
travail and agonizing that attend all serious efforts toward unity are
no incidental part of the story: they are signs of the presence and
working of a power that holds its servants to a task that does all

manner of violence to their natural tastes and interests. By it they
have been given patience to listen to long expositions of doctrinal
points that seemed to them inconsequential—and the greater patience
to try to understand why some of their brethren regard these issues
as momentous. They have endured the disappointment and frustration of seeing supposed agreements vanish with the discovery that
the very terms in which these painfully wrought agreements were
expressed carried radically different meanings for different persons.
They have been given grace to expose and re-expose themselves to
the most searching kind of mutual questioning, which in any other
setting would be construed as skepticism concerning the sincerity of
their Christian discipleship. They have come to a place of apparent
mutual acceptance where all seemed willing to concede that other
communions have borne faithful witness to Christ and are therefore
to be recognized as authentic churches, only to discover such grave
reservations (e.g., the *vestigia ecclesiae* business mentioned in Chapter IV) as to call in question the whole assumption. Yet in the midst
of these tensions and testings they have known that they were men
under constraint. They have known they were not permitted to turn
their backs on one another, for in so doing they would be turning
away from Christ. This was clearly said by the Edinburgh Conference:

> We are one in faith in our Lord Jesus Christ, the incarnate Word of
> God. . . . We are one in acknowledging that this allegiance takes
> precedence of any other allegiance that may make claims upon us. . . .
> We humbly acknowledge that our divisions are contrary to the will of
> Christ, and we pray God in His mercy to shorten the days of our separa-
> tion and to guide us by His Spirit into fulness of unity.[7]

It was reiterated at Amsterdam in even more resonant terms, and
now with the humbling but reassuring experience of another twenty
years of ecumenical effort behind the declaration:

> We are divided from one another not only in matters of faith, order,
> and traditions, but also by pride of nation, class, and race. But Christ has
> made us His own, and He is not divided. In seeking Him we find one
> another. . . . We intend to stay together.[8]

Evanston reaffirmed all this, and went further. The Report of the
Advisory Commission, preparatory to the Assembly, was more

realistic, more rigorous in its analysis of the problems of unity, and more restrained in its estimate of the tempo of advance than any previous official utterances of the World Council. Yet it was no less positive in affirming that the churches participating in the Council are under mandate to an imperative—from which they cannot now release themselves even if they would—to continue the struggle for the unity that outwardly evades them but inwardly will not let them go. The Commission said:

> In our separateness we have attested the operation of the one Christ across all boundaries that divide us. We have heard the voice of the Good Shepherd in the testimony of communions other than our own. We have experienced the power of the Name of Christ in their prayers. We have acknowledged the love of Christ to which they have borne witness in word and deed. In the fellowship of the Ecumenical Movement we have come together in a way which forbids us, in spite of all stresses, to break away from one another. Thus we have been led to see that the reality of Christ is more comprehensive than the limits of our confessional traditions, and have confessed in faith our oneness in Christ.[9]

The fact that the churches, in the midst of their humiliating confession of the sins of disunity—indeed, because they have been given grace to make this confession—are able to say, "Christ has made us His own," is a sign of God's mighty working that needs to be proclaimed in preaching.

A still greater wonder is the new readiness of churches to say of other communions, "Christ has made them His own." All this, as John Marsh affirms, is authentic good news.

> Is not one of the most amazing mysteries of the life of the Church that, in its dreadful and sinful dividing of Christ's body, He has never disowned any of us, but that we all, precisely in our separate and therefore mutilated bodies still bear some marks of His "communion" with us, both in and outside the Sacrament of the Lord's Supper? Now it seems to a Reformed churchman that in a Church so divided, this deep unity, which is nothing less than Christ Himself as the deep reality of all the Churches' life, is "gospel" or good news. And being such, it is something which has to be "proclaimed" or "preached." [10]

Second, preaching that communicates the dynamic of the New

Reformation will mediate the judgment of the Church on our churches.

There is a Church of Jesus Christ that transcends the churches, that stands over them in judgment. Through the Ecumenical Movement we have been permitted to glimpse its lineaments and dimensions. This vision of the Church is today a primary mediator of God's judgment on our existing churches. We dare not shield ourselves and our congregations from what the Spirit is saying to the churches— through the Church.

The fact that there is a whole Church of Christ standing over against the churches, in judgment and in promise, needs to be preached in plain language. The present structure of the organized Ecumenical Movement tends to conceal this truth. Much emphasis is placed on the character of the World Council of Churches as a creature of the member communions; it is constituted by official representatives of the denominations and is responsible to the denominations. From these structural facts the inference may readily be drawn that the Ecumenical Movement is subordinate to the denominations, that it is spiritually accountable to them, and that the denominations are entitled—each from its own vantage point— to pass judgment on it.

It is clear, however, that the dynamics of the Ecumenical Movement have burst its structural bonds. The World Council of Churches, as its officers and published statements repeatedly declare, *is not the Church.* Yet the Council has no reason for existence if it does not exist *to bear witness to the Church.* And one must go on to say very plainly that at crucial points its witness is more adequate and faithful than that of the member denominations. It is because of this witness-bearing character that the Ecumenical Movement, of which the World Council is the most important organ, compels the churches (though it has no power of compulsion save the authority of that to which it testifies) to expose their life to scrutiny and judgment in the light of the Church.

This doubtless explains—at least in part—why the World Council has felt obliged to be so insistent and specific (and, some of us feel, so gratuitous) in disclaiming every interpretation of its function that would allow it to be confused with the Church. "It is not a Super-

Church. It is not the World Church. It is not the Una Sancta of which the Creeds speak." [11] This should be so obvious as to need no explication. Yet there remains the fact (and it must be disturbing to many churches) that when the Council mediates the judgment of the Church on the churches it almost *becomes* the Church in one of its modes. Because it is so close to being the Church—and in exactly the form that is most uncomfortable for the churches in their separation—the churches will continue to experience seasons of uneasiness about it, and the Council will accordingly feel obliged to enter further disclaimers.

The vision of the Church vouchsafed through the Ecumenical Movement has authority over the churches not merely because it reveals a Church restored to unity—as though this were the sole distinguishing mark of a Living Church—but because it is the place where those concerns and dedications that give evidence of the Church's true livingness are most strongly converging. More and more the World Council of Churches, the International Missionary Council, the commissions and committees where men and women labor arduously over plans for the union of separated churches, are becoming the rallying places for members of the Christian community who are most wholeheartedly committed to the Church's mission and reformation. Here are gathered those who are giving heart and strength to the whole range of interests involved in the Church's service and obedience to its Lord: those who in theological and biblical study are reflecting most intensely upon the meaning of the Christian faith; those who are most passionately concerned for the mission of the Church, that its faith shall be proclaimed in word and life; those most engrossed in the work of evangelism and the penetration of society with the reconciling love and power of the Cross. It is this "gathered Church"—gathered by the Christ who when He calls men to Himself calls them into membership of one another—that stands over against the churches in judgment and in promise. The fact that it is *there*—that the vision of it and the foretaste of it are in a profound way the actualization of it—is something to be preached.

For the preacher this reality of the Church in its wholeness, now coming into visibility in the Ecumenical Movement, is both a responsibility and a resource. It is a responsibility because there is no likelihood that the great Church will ever come into vital and creative relationship with the local congregation unless it is given access to the local church through preaching. It is a resource because the relating of the local fellowship to the life of the great Church is a fundamental objective of Christian preaching. Indeed, there is a profound sense in which the invasion of the local church by the life of the great Church in all its amplitude, and the leading of the members of the local church into fullness of membership in the great Church, are the whole task and purpose to which the minister is commissioned. Says Daniel Jenkins:

The chief way in which the Ecumenical Movement should be influencing churches and in which churches should be expressing their allegiance to it is, therefore, in the way their minister preaches the Word and dispenses the Sacraments. The interesting suggestion has been made that our Lord's commission to His disciples at the end of St. Matthew's Gospel, "Go ye therefore and make disciples of all nations," might reasonably be translated, "Go ye therefore and make disciples ecumenically." That is to say, the reference is not so much to the geographical area, or to the people which the proclamation should address, but to the manner in which it should be made. If we are to fulfill our Lord's command, it is in this way that the Gospel should be proclaimed in particular churches. It is a public Gospel offered to all mankind, and has authority for the whole of life. If a particular church is to hold communion of heart and mind with Christ and His Great Church, it must hear and obey that Gospel in its own place. In that purpose it needs the help of a gifted and learned minister. If he is faithful to his calling, he will see the Ecumenical Movement not as an optional extra on the fringe of the church, an interesting activity for those who have the time and inclination to attend conferences and to pursue new ideas, but as an instrument sent by God for helping him to fulfill his own most central tasks the more effectively in his own place.[12]

It is doubtless one of the most distinctive signs of a revolutionary time that in the life of the churches—as in political and economic life—we are now called to submit to judgment by movements and orders we have helped to initiate and shape. The churches of the West, for example, now confront the so-called younger churches born of the missionary endeavor, and are obliged to confess that these newer churches, especially because of their determined struggle for and achievement of a more inclusive unity, are in many ways bearing a more faithful testimony to the Gospel than are their parent churches of the Western world. We need grace to subject ourselves to their scrutiny, and to the judgment of the Church that they mediate. Can all of us, together with the Anglicans who were directly addressed, hear with humility the word of the Church of South India? When the South India churchmen were asked by the Anglicans to make known their ultimate intention as regards ministerial orders, whether at the end of the agreed-upon period of thirty years their ministry will be "regularized" from the viewpoint of Anglicanism, they answered:

We are united in one Church; our parent Churches are divided. If it is now insisted that we state what our permanent relation with them is to be, we can only say that we can be content with nothing except that they should be united as we are. So long as they remain divided our position must remain anomalous from the point of view of any one of the divided Churches. But from the point of view of the historic faith of the Church we must surely judge that the real anomaly, the real scandal, is that the Church should be divided. We have promised at the end of 30 years to give equal weight to two principles; that our own ministry shall be one and that we shall maintain and extend full communion with our parent Churches. As things stand, these two principles are irreconcilable. They can only be reconciled when the parent Churches now divided are united. Our act of union is an act of faith in the Holy Spirit that He will bring this about. We cannot therefore say more than the Constitution has said about what our successors will do in circumstances which we pray may be profoundly different from those in which we now are.[13]

Reading that statement, and remembering that its authors knew that the support of their missionary church by one of its parent bodies would be greatly affected by their reply, one submits that this body of so-called younger churches has pretty well grown up!

It is this kind of judgment, of the churches by the Church—the Church that exists not merely as vision but as increasing actualization —that we are called to mediate in preaching.

Third, the new Reformation will be preached as our preaching becomes an instrument for helping the local congregation find and realize the distinctiveness of its life as a people of God.

Reinhold Niebuhr has pointed out the tragedy of sectarianism in the fact that whereas nearly all the sects came into existence with the purpose of sharpening the distinction between the Church and the world, the effect of sectarianism has been to blur that distinction. By the dissipation of the *integrity* of the Church the *distinctiveness* of the Church is also dissipated.

Our churches have to realize anew their identity as a people. This requires, in part, that they be continually reminded of those common memories that are theirs as a community—that are much more than memories because they are dynamically present in their life today.

In the book of Deuteronomy there is a word of Moses spoken to the Children of Israel. In it he is simply reminding them who they are. He is saying in substance: "Until you remember and understand this past that I am bringing to your mind, you do not know yourselves. You do not know who you are. You are anonymous; you are nameless, faceless, without identity. You are merely a crowd of individuals who happen to be in the same place. And as individuals you are less than persons. You have no real name."

Something like this Moses might have said if he had spoken in the generalities common to our forms of speech. But since the writers of the Bible had no interest in generalities and were always incorrigibly specific, what Moses actually said to the Children of Israel was this: "The Lord took you, and lifted you out of the iron furnace, out of Egypt, to be unto him a people of inheritance." This is who you are. Apart from this inheritance you are no people. You are no one. What makes you someone—what constitutes you a people with a name, and a history, and a present existence, and a promise, is precisely this: that the Lord took you up, and brought you out, and chose you, and made you a people of inheritance.

This, of course, is a recurrent theme in the Bible. Indeed, we may almost say that it is *the* theme—the master-motif that runs through the whole Book. It is repeated in a thousand varying forms. It declares that the people of Israel and the history of Israel are important, not because Israel is a great people, or a strong people, or a righteous people, or even—as we used to be fond of saying—a people "with a genius for religion." Israel is important—indeed Israel is a people at all—simply and solely because it is a *chosen* people. In the history of this strange community—which is still a profound mystery among the nations of earth—God has taken the initiative and has entered into a covenant relationship: God has *called* this people to fulfill a purpose. This purpose is that He may declare Himself in His character of Deliverer and Redeemer.

All the memories of Israel go back to an act of deliverance. We were slaves in Egypt, and the Lord delivered us out of the hands of the Egyptians, and brought us out of the house of bondage. The one sin behind all sins is to forget this inheritance or to misunderstand it. It is for Israel to imagine that she was chosen because she deserved to be chosen. It is to imagine that she came to the Promised Land because she was worthy of it, and to forget that she received it simply because God gave it to her.

The same theme runs through the New Testament. But now the "people of inheritance" is the new Israel, the Church of Jesus Christ. And the one thing the members of the Church must never forget is that the new life of hope and joy and power has come to them not because of their merit and deserving but as a gift. In the life and sacrifice of Christ, God has come to us and has given us a part in that victory.

So the heart of the Church's testimony is in that hymn of praise in the First Epistle of Peter:

Blessed be the God and Father of our Lord Jesus Christ. By his great mercy we have been born anew to a living hope through the resurrection of Jesus Christ from the dead, unto an inheritance incorruptible, undefiled, and that fadeth not away . . .

It is an inheritance—something *given* to us, not something we have fashioned or done. The supreme evidence of it is something we never *could* have done—the resurrection of Christ from the dead.

Being conscious of an inheritance is no backward-looking act of piety toward the past; it is that reappropriation of a distinctive life that is a part of all reformation.

Here is added reason for insistence on the necessity for preaching that is essentially and solidly biblical in character. The Bible is the account of God's dealings with His people. Our membership in this people, our sense of participation in and continuity with its distinctive life, depend on our knowing that its story is also our story. We are coming to understand that the whole task of Christian education is essentially not the communication of facts or ideas or even attitudes, but the initiation of persons into the life of this distinctive community, with its memories, its faith, and its hopes.

The act of "bringing to remembrance," which is not merely recalling a past but repossessing a common life that is also dynamically in the present, is one of the modes of reformation. We have to preach in such a way that by the Word to which we testify the people of Christ are recalled and regathered. As a condition of being reformed, we who belong to this people are in need of being informed as to who we are—a community brought into being by a deed. This deed was not done for us alone, but the knowledge of it, given us by faith, is what makes us a people.

One of the fears repeatedly expressed about church union is that it can be accomplished only by a weakening of the quality of existing loyalties—a loosening of the bonds of fellowship and commitment that exist in our separate communions. I do not believe that anxiety is justified as long as we keep a firm grasp on the principle that union is not to be accomplished merely by mechanical adjustment and organizational reconstruction. Union will come as the Church is led to be more a distinctive people, not less—and as it becomes more truly a people it will learn that it is one people. It will learn that it is required to become more and more one people if it is to be at all a distinguishable people in the modern world.

We have noted that very frequently the first consequence of ecumenical meeting and discussion is to make the participants more vividly conscious of their own separate traditions and practices. In the course of interpreting their own ways to others they often find themselves forced to a position of defending their ways—sometimes with a certain aggressiveness they seldom display outside such conversations. This tendency, when it comes at one stage of the ecumenical encounters, seems to me thoroughly wholesome. What obstructs the union of the churches more than loyalty to our separate communities is the lack of awareness of any distinctively Christian community. The need is for a genuine recovery of identity, even if it be for a time a sense of identity that is mediated through the denomination. But the primary agency of such recovery is of course the life of the local congregation.

Moreover, this must be a real recovery, a reappropriation of the profounder meanings of the corporate life.

In my own denomination, the Congregational Christian Churches, we have been engaged in an arduous and sometimes painful search for this fundamental kind of self-knowledge. The occasion for it has been the development of plans and the taking of appropriate actions preparatory to union with the Evangelical and Reformed Church. In this connection we have had a decade of continuous and lively debate between the prounion majority and a dissenting minority. We have had a long legal action in the civil courts, instigated by opponents of the union in an attempt to prevent its consummation. We have had a Commission on Free Church Polity and Christian Unity, examining our polity with the particular interest of trying to discover what actions are required, and by what body or bodies they may properly be taken, for a fellowship of churches that has no agency of general government to do the things necessary to unite itself with another communion. Much of this process of debate and self-scrutiny has not been entirely comfortable. Yet in the midst of it we have known that other denominations must eventually undergo the same disturbance and testing as they become increasingly aware of the implications of the ecumenical encounter for their own life, and particularly when they consider (as we have been doing) actual church union outside the conventional alliances of denominational families. Indeed this sequence of experiences is recognized as normal: a heightening of interdenominational consciousness is followed by an accentuation of denominational self-consciousness. This may and not infrequently does take the form of a fresh outburst of enthusiasm for programs of denominational expansionism. It may also have a more creative and ecumenically fruitful outcome. Provided it is radical enough, and is pressed far enough, this endeavor toward self-understanding and awareness of identity as a distinct people may actually result in placing the denomination more securely in the life of the great Church.

But this "provided" is all-important. It means getting underneath the secondary characteristics and differentia, and uncovering the basic loyalties and convictions—which are always more profound and universal than their particular expressions, which were shaped by special circumstances of history. For my own denomination, for example, this means going behind the manuals on organizations, the codifications of practices, the handbooks on what is called among us "the law of Congregational usage." It means a search for the spiritual dynamics of our life—for the fundamental concerns and devotions that called us into being as a people. It means especially a return to the primary sources and historic origins of our denominational existence. P. T. Forsyth has strikingly pointed out why the normative period for a denomination—as for the Christian Church itself—is its beginning.

The more spiritual any historic movement is, *i.e.*, the more dependent on revelation, so much the more it must return always to its classic source to adjust its compass, and to realise its genius and its call. And the more spiritual it is the more also it will be found to have its classic and normative time at its source. Its principle is in its creation, like human freedom; which being given by God, was given for God. The more spiritual it is the more is it of positive inspiration. And the inspiration of historic religions is chiefly with their founders or their foundation. The case is otherwise with movements which are but evolutionary. There the process works up from beneath instead of down from above. We have then to do with a mere development and not a revelation. So that we may find the law or principle in the finished product more clearly and powerfully than at the point of origin. . . . But it is not so that we learn Christ. He is not a great step in a greater process, not the hand at the sluice that releases a greater power than it possesses; but He is Himself the fountainhead of all that religion can ever be for man and for his soul. It is to Him, therefore, and to the apostles He chose and inspired for His self-revelation, that the Church they created must ever return for the standard, as for the power, whereby it is to go on and minister to each age as it arrives.

If it is so with the whole Church, it is so also with each great movement within the Church itself which recalls it to its true mission and genius. In developing such movements we must, in proportion as they are spiritual, profound, and regal for an age—we must return to their first spring, and to the apostolic men in whom they rose to power and effect. There we have the principle in its true purity and force. There it was most deeply and clearly grasped.[14]

When the process of denominational self-scrutiny is radical enough and takes the form of a return to the true sources of a communion's life, then it may have ecumenically positive results. A denomination like my own is compelled to ask: To what were our fathers really witnessing when our separate community began? Did they come apart in the interest of diminishing or weakening the fullness of the Christian faith, or for the purpose of offering, as they believed, a more complete testimony and obedience to that faith? Was it in order to embody in their life something *less* than the wholeness of the Church, or was it to reassert that wholeness, which they believed had been disfigured? And to what, precisely, in our fathers' testimony ought we to feel bound today? Are we called to perpetuate their *opinions*, their *views*—mistaken or correct, historically conditioned and contingent as they so obviously were? Or is our true inheritance their faith in Christ and their purpose to be obedient to Him? And is it necessary, in our day, that this testimony to the faith of our fathers—not to the opinions of our fathers—should be given from outside an avowed and increasingly realized corporate membership in the common life of the people of Christ?

It is not by weakening the binding power and conviction of these actual historic communities in which we dwell that union will come, but by returning to their primary sources and finding that they are indeed the one source.

In our preaching of the new Reformation we are to preach for the reconstituting of the Church in its distinctiveness as a people—as the body of Christ.

In our day we are called to make the unity of the Church not only a matter of concern but of unremitting and dedicated effort. Yet we are never to suppose, as we carry on this labor, that it will come primarily as a consequence of our toil. When Luther returned to Wittenberg after his exile in the Wartburg he spoke to the people there about the beginnings and course of the Reformation. He said:

All I have done is to further, preach, and teach God's Word; otherwise I have done nothing. So it happened that while I slept, or while I had a glass of beer with my friend Philip [Melanchthon] and with Amsdorf, the papacy was so weakened as it never was before by the action of any prince or emperor. I have done nothing; the Word has done and accomplished everything. . . . I let the Word do its work.[15]

We also are to let the Word do its reconciling work, to regather the Church.

Fourth, the new Reformation is preached wherever the mission of the Church is set forth in its wholeness and urgency.

We shall misread the meaning of events if we think it is entirely due to outward circumstances surrounding the church on the mission field—to its minority status and the opposition of an openly hostile culture—that the churches in mission lands have found their unity much more rapidly than the churches of the West. There is another fact—and it is primary—that in the younger churches the sense of mission is quick and powerful. Bishop Newbigin of the Church of South India is very confident that this is the dynamic behind the achievement of union there; and it is the lack of it that is the retarding factor explaining our slowness here. He says:

It is not possible to account for the contentment with the divisions of the Church except upon the basis of a loss of conviction that the Church exists to bring all men to Christ. There is the closest possible connection between the acceptance of the missionary obligation and the acceptance of the obligation of unity. That which makes the Church one is what makes it a mission to the world.[16]

For the preacher, this seems to me to mean that the reformation of our church life is dependent on something of which preaching is only the indirect servant; and this statement would be incomplete without reference to it. Preaching in its full significance is possible only in the context of the Church's full life—which includes the continuous and concrete identification of the Church with the anguish and misery and injustice and brokenness of the world, and a ministry to that brokenness. Says one of the Amsterdam papers:

Preaching, divorced from concern with all men's needs will be words against deeds, for men will not believe the message of God's grace if they do not see signs of that grace in the messengers. Service of men divorced from preaching will be but mocking men with false hopes, for there is no place other than the Cross where men may be reconciled to God, and every man must go there himself.[17]

We need to remember when we are considering the fullness of the Church's life in terms of its order, for example, that there is another kind of fullness that may be called "functional," and that from the beginning has been a necessary mark of catholicity. In the Church at its start there were always these three elements: kerygma —its proclamation; koinonia—the fellowship of the people of Christ; and diakonia—simple service to the needs of men.

And it is the sense of the tragic impairment of the Church's capacity to render an acceptable and relevant service amid the complexities of our time that becomes one source of steady—and ultimately irresistible—pressure toward unity. In our preaching there will have to be this word of realism concerning our impotence vis-a-vis the world.

It is speaking falsely to disguise this impotence by the celebration of the "great achievements" of interdenominational co-operation—by speaking of the National Council of Churches as a great step toward unity. Some of us who believe in the National Council and give an unconscionable amount of time and effort to its interests, nevertheless regard much of this labor as a work of penance for the sins that consign us to co-operation instead of visible and effective unity. The interdenominational enterprise, in which are invested enormous toil and skill in the operation of vast organizations—very often for the negative purpose of agreeing to keep out of each other's way—is not the Church of Christ finding its oneness.

We publish brochures on what the denominations are putting into the co-operative effort, but we do not talk about how much more is withheld. When we praise the advance of "comity," we do not speak of the times when comity agreements are broken—and not infrequently with the connivance of the officials who have helped to make them. In fact the very notion of comity, and especially the pretensions of notable accomplishment that are frequently attached to it, deserve the blunt challenge of a plain-speaking Christian from the East. "As to comity," says D. T. Niles, "this is simply an arrangement whereby divorced parents have provided that their children should not suffer unduly." [18] I have myself spoken in public about how admirable it is that in the Division of Home Missions in the National Council of Churches the denominations have gone beyond the state of merely talking things over, and have actually assigned to the co-operative agency responsibility for certain tasks in the field. But I am afraid I have not always made it clear that the projects surrendered by the denominations are mainly among such ecclesiastically unprofitable groups as share-croppers, migrants, and Indians on reservations.

The note of penitence for the laggardness of our service to mankind—and for the more disastrous failure to confront the economic, political, and international order with any clear witness by the Church of Christ concerning the requirements of social redemption —ought to be a part of the Church's confession and cry for mercy and leading that are uttered in the preached word. It will also be a safeguard against the capture of our concern for unity by a churchmanship that is essentially introverted, that views the struggle toward unity as being primarily for the sake of the Church's institutional prosperity and success. As Evanston reminded us:

. . . The unity given to the Church in Christ, and gifts given to the Church to help and enable it to manifest its given unity, are not for the sake of the Church as an historical society, but for the sake of the world. The Church has its being and its unity in the "Son of Man, who came not to be ministered unto, but to minister and to give his life a ransom for many." The being and unity of the Church belong to Christ and therefore to His mission, to His enduring the Cross for the joy that was set before Him. Christ wrought "one new man" for us all by His death, and it is by entering into His passion for the redemption of a sinful and divided world that the Church finds its unity in its crucified and risen Lord.[19]

Reference has been made to a book by Father A. G. Hebert called *The Form of the Church*. It discusses many questions of order, the ministry, and sacramental life. But there is one omission that is all the more strange because of the very title of the book; a reference to the Epistle to the Philippians would have been helpful. There Paul pleads with the Philippians that they shall be united— "that ye be likeminded, having the same love, being of one accord, of one mind." But what is the ground of this accord, this unity? It is this:

Let this mind be in you which was also in Christ Jesus: who being in the form of God thought it not robbery to be equal with God: but made himself of no reputation, and took upon him the *form of a servant*, and was made in the likeness of man: and being found in fashion as a man, he humbled himself, and became obedient unto death, even the death of the cross.

Granted that the idea of "service" may be terribly sentimentalized and trivialized. Granted that it may become service in the way the world wishes to be served rather than redemptive service after the pattern of Christ's own action. But it is impossible to think of the form and fullness of the Church—of its truly "showing forth" Christ's life and death, except as it knows and follows its vocation to exist in the form of a servant.

But in this also preaching has a more than ancillary place. It is the most direct form of service the Church has to give. By means of it, when it rises to its full, august, and catholic majesty, the Church is forever presenting itself to its Christ and offering itself for renewal and employment as His Body. In the same act of preaching, the Church also performs the direct and supreme service of offering its Christ to the world. It deliberately seeks to place itself in the ageless apostolic situation, wherein it actively seeks its own continual reformation that it may be faithful in its apostolic and missionary calling. The Church exists for the Good News. Preaching is the Sacrament by which the Church offers the Good News to the world.

Notes

Foreword

[1] Karl Barth, *The Word of God and the Word of Man* (trans. Douglas Horton), Boston, Pilgrim Press, 1928, p. 97.

[2] John Baillie and Hugh Martin (eds.), *Revelation*, New York, Macmillan, 1937, p. 1.

Chapter I

[1] Robert S. Bilheimer, *What Must the Church Do?* New York, Harper, 1947, pp. 63–64, 80.

[2] J. H. Nichols, *Evanston: An Interpretation*, New York, Harper, 1954, p. 7.

[3] So far as I have been able to learn it was Robert Bilheimer, secretary of the Study Department of the World Council of Churches, who first characterized the Ecumenical Movement as a modern reformation. Since the time when these lectures were given, Charles Clayton Morrison has published his Hoover Lectures on Christian Unity under the title, *The Unfinished Reformation* (New York, Harper, 1953).

[4] Cf. article in *Theology Today*, Vol. IV, No. 4, Jan., 1948.

[5] Leonard Hodgson (ed.), *The Second World Conference on Faith and Order*, New York, Macmillan, 1938, pp. 359–60.

[6] William Temple, *The Church Looks Forward*, New York, Macmillan, 1944.

[7] Oliver Tomkins, *The Wholeness of the Church*, London, SCM Press, 1949, p. 43.

[8] *The Universal Church in God's Design* (Amsterdam Series, Vol. I), New York, Harper, 1948, pp. 185, 188.

[9] Hodgson (ed.), *op. cit.*, p. 55.

[10] Tomkins, *op. cit.*, pp. 110–11.

[11] New York, Harper, 1948.

[12] R. N. Flew and R. E. Davies (eds.), London, Lutterworth, 1950.

[13] In *Christianity and Crisis*, Vol. VII, No. 20, Nov. 24, 1947, pp. 5–7.

Chapter II

[1] *Man's Disorder and God's Design*, New York, Harper, 1949, Vol. III, p. 195.

[2] W. A. Visser 't Hooft (ed.), *The Evanston Report*, New York, Harper, 1955, p. 90.

[3] Lesslie Newbigin, *The Reunion of the Church*, New York, Harper, 1949, p. 136.

[4] *The Bible and the Church's Message*, Study Department of the World Council of Churches, 1949, p. 14.

[5] Cf. Walter M. Horton, *Toward a Reborn Church*, New York, Harper, 1949, pp. 109–10.

[6] Barth, op. cit., pp. 100–103.

[7] *The Bible and the Church's Message*, p. 8.

[8] *Ibid.*

[9] Alan Richardson and Wolfgang Schweitzer (eds.), *Biblical Authority for Today*, Philadelphia, Westminster, 1951, pp. 212–13.

[10] John Marsh, in *ibid.*, pp. 188–89.

[11] Daniel T. Jenkins, *The Gift of Ministry*, London, Faber, 1947, p. 32.

CHAPTER III

[1] P. T. Forsyth, *Positive Preaching and the Modern Mind*, London, Independent Press, 1907, p. 53.

[2] *Ibid.*, p. 58.

[3] *Ibid.*, pp. 59–60.

[4] Jenkins, *The Church Meeting and Democracy*, London, Independent Press, 1944, pp. 35–36.

[5] Rudolf Bultmann, calling attention to the fact that when Paul speaks of the Lord's Supper as a "proclaiming" of the Lord's death (I Cor. 11:26) he uses the same word he employs elsewhere for preaching, remarks that this "indicates that the Sacrament of the Lord's Supper like that of baptism is also co-ordinate with the word proclamation and ultimately only a special mode of it." *Theology of the New Testament* (trans. K. Grobel), New York, Scribner's, 1951, Vol. I, pp. 312–13.

[6] H. F. Lovell Cocks, *By Faith Alone*, London, James Clarke, 1943, p. 113. Since this was written Henry Sloane Coffin has published his cogent and helpful study of the close relationship between the Word and the Sacraments, *Communion Through Preaching*, New York, Scribner's, 1952.

[7] *Ibid.*, pp. 113–14.

[8] *Report of the Commission on Ways of Worship.*

[9] Theodore O. Wedel, "The Great Vacuum in Christian Theology," *Theology Today*, Vol. II, No. 1, p. 37.

[10] R. K. Orchard, *The Open Bible*, London, Independent Press, 1943, p. 31.

[11] C. H. Dodd, *History and the Gospel*, New York, Scribner's, 1938, p. 150.

[12] Wilhelm Pauck, *The Heritage of the Reformation*, Boston, Beacon Press, 1950, pp. 5–6.

[13] Cf. J. T. McNeill, *Unitive Protestantism*, Nashville, Abingdon, 1930, pp. 63–65.

[14] John Calvin, *Institutes of the Christian Religion* (trans. John Allen), Philadelphia, Presbyterian Board of Publication, 1911, Vol. II, p. 224.

[15] Flew and Davies (eds.), *op. cit.*, pp. 91–92.

[16] *Christendom*, Vol. IX, No. 2, pp. 284, 286–87.

[17] "A Message from the Second Assembly of the World Council of Churches," *The Evanston Report*, pp. 1, 3.

Chapter IV

[1] *The Missionary Obligation of the Church*, London, Edinburgh House, 1952, pp. 6–7.

[2] G. K. A. Bell, *Documents on Christian Unity: Third Series, 1930–48*, London, Oxford University Press, 1948, pp. 222–23.

[3] Cf. H. P. Van Dusen, *World Christianity*, Nashville, Abingdon, 1947, pp. 216, 222–23.

[4] Newbigin, *op. cit.*, p. 167.

[5] Flew and Davies (eds.), *op. cit.*, p. 21.

[6] Oliver Tomkins, *The Wholeness of the Church*, London, SCM Press, 1949, p. 54.

[7] *The Universal Church in God's Design*, Amsterdam Series, Vol. I, p. 207.

[8] "A Message from the Second Assembly of the World Council of Churches."

[9] *The Universal Church in God's Design*, Vol. I, p. 205.

[10] Van Dusen, in *Christendom*, Vol. III, No. 3, p. 255.

[11] *The Universal Church in God's Design*, Vol. I, p. 205.

[12] *Ecumenical Review*, Vol. III, No. 3, p. 216.

[13] Horton, *op. cit.*, pp. 95–96.

[14] McNeill, *op. cit.*, pp. 85–88.

[15] A. G. Hebert, *The Form of the Church*, London, Faber, 1944, p. 64.

[16] *Ibid.*, p. 120.

[17] *Ibid.*, pp. 120–21.

[18] Van Dusen, *World Christianity*, p. 226.

[19] Various writers, *Catholicity*, London, Dacre, 1947, p. 44.

[20] Van Dusen, "The Issues of Christian Unity," in *Christendom*, Vol. XI, No. 3, p. 340.

[21] *The Evanston Report*, pp. 88, 89.

[22] R. Newton Flew (ed.), *The Nature of the Church*, New York, Harper, 1952, p. 165.

[23] *The Evanston Report*, p. 89.

[24] Forsyth, in *Towards Reunion* (by various writers), London, Macmillan, 1919, pp. 58–60.

CHAPTER V

[1] Cocks, *op. cit.*, pp. 114–15.

[2] T. S. Eliot, *The Idea of a Christian Society*, New York, Harcourt, Brace, 1940, p. 21.

[3] Cf. J. A. Brandt, "Intellectual Slave Market," in *Saturday Review of Literature*, June 5, 1948, p. 20.

[4] *The Evanston Report*, p. 29.

[5] S. Kierkegaard, *Journals* (ed. and trans. Alexander Dru), London, Oxford, 1938, Entry No. 1305, p. 498.

[6] *The Church's Witness to God's Design* (Amsterdam Series, Vol. II), New York, Harper, 1948, p. 201.

[7] Julian N. Hartt, *Toward a Theology of Evangelism*, Nashville, Abingdon, 1955, p. 113.

[8] Cf. J. McConnachie, *Reformation Old and New* (ed. F. W. Camfield), London, Lutterworth, 1947, p. 104.

[9] Forsyth, *Positive Preaching and the Modern Mind*, pp. 197–98.

[10] G. Ernest Wright in *Biblical Authority for Today*.

[11] *Christendom*, Vol. XII, No. 3, p. 298.

[12] Barth, *The Word of God and the Word of Man*, p. 216.

CHAPTER VI

[1] Max Warren, *The Christian Mission*, London, SCM Press, 1951, pp. 11–12.

[2] Tomkins, *op. cit.*, p. 42.

[3] For a description of the early Church as "The Eschatological Congregation" cf. Bultmann, *op. cit.*, especially pp. 37–42, 306–13.

[4] M. G. Lagny, quoted in *Faith and Order*, Official Report, 1937, p. 212.

[5] Oliver Tomkins, *op. cit.*, p. 11.

[6] Daniel T. Jenkins, "The Congregational Ministry in an Ecumenical Setting," *The Congregational Ministry in the Modern World* (ed. H. Cunliffe-Jones), London, Independent Press, 1955, p. 18.

[7] Leonard Hodgson (ed.), *Faith and Order: Edinburgh 1937*, New York, Macmillan, 1938, p. 275.

[8] Visser 't Hooft (ed.), *The First Assembly of the World Council of Churches*, New York, Harper, 1949, p. 9.

[9] *The Christian Hope and the Task of the Church*, Report of the Advisory Commission on the Main Theme of the Second Assembly, New York, Harper, 1954, p. 20.

[10] Donald Baillie and John Marsh (eds.), *Intercommunion*, New York, Harper, 1952, p. 279.

[11] *The Christian Hope and the Task of the Church*, p. 10.

[12] Jenkins, in *The Congregational Ministry in the Modern World*, p. 23.

[13] *The Church of South India*, London, Church Information Board, 1950, pp. 37–38.

[14] Forsyth, *Faith, Freedom, and the Future*, New York, Hodder & Stoughton, 1912, pp. 344–45.

[15] Pauck, *op. cit.*, p. 23.

[16] Newbigin, *op. cit.*, p. 11.

[17] Vol. II, p. 32.

[18] *Ecumenical Review*, Vol. V, No. 3, p. 245.

[19] *The Evanston Report*, p. 85.

Index

Abraham, 49

Advisory Commission, Report of the, 117; quoted, 118

Allen, John, 135

Amsterdam, ix, 2, 5, 17, 64, 65, 67, 96, 116, 117, 129

Amsterdam Series, 91, 101; quoted, 5, 64, 96, 129

Anabaptists, 52

Anglican, 9, 12, 30, 57, 59, 60, 73, 74, 75, 105, 122

Anglo-Catholic, 11, 12, 51, 66, 70, 73, 74, 75, 76, 82

Apostles, 21, 71

Archbishop of Canterbury, 66, 116

Arian, 105

Augustine, 48, 50

Axioms of the Modern Man, 102

Azariah, V. S., 9

Baillie, Donald M., quoted, 118

Baillie, John, quoted, x

Baptism, 43, 71, 72

Baptist, 30, 71, 79, 80

Barth, Karl, x, 11, 21, 22, 23, 24, 35, 94, 99, 107, 108

"Barthians," 22

Bell, G. K. A., quoted, 58

Berdyaev, Nicholas, 11

Between Hocking and Kraemer, 101

Bible and the Church's Message, The, quoted, 21, 27, 31

Biblical Authority for Today, xii; quoted, 32, 33, 104

Bilheimer, Robert S., xvi, 133

Bossey, 21

Brandt, J. A., quoted, 93

Broadcasting and Film Commission, 101

Brunner, Emil, 10, 11, 108

Bultmann, Rudolf, 134; quoted, 43, 112

By Faith Alone, quoted, 43, 90

Calvin, John, xvi, 51

Calvinist, 21, 52, 67

Camfield, F. W., 136

Canada, United Church of, 59

Catholic, 85, 86, 107

Catholicism, 69, 76, 82

Catholicity, quoted, 74

Catholicity of Protestantism, The, 12, 52; quoted, 63

Ceylon, 59

Christendom, quoted, 53, 65, 77, 105

Christian Hope and the Task of the Church, The, quoted, 118, 120

Christian Message in a Non-Christian World, The, 101

Christian Mission, The, quoted, 110

Christian Witness in a Revolutionary World, The, 95

Christianity and Crisis, quoted, 13

Church Looks Forward, The, quoted, 3

Church Meeting, 40

Church Meeting and Democracy, The, quoted, 41

Church of England, 52, 71

Church's Witness to God's Design, The, 101; quoted, 96

Cocks, H. F. Lovell, 43, 90, 109

Coffin, Henry Sloane, 134

Commission on Free Church Polity and Christian Unity, 126

Communications Research Project, 101

Communion through Preaching, 134

Confession of Faith, 15

Congregational, 67, 70, 72, 73, 85, 127

Congregational Christian Churches, 126

Congregational Ministry in an Ecumenical Setting, The, quoted, 115

Congregational Ministry in the Modern World, The, quoted, 115, 121

Congregationalism, 6

Congregationalist, 30, 40, 60, 66, 67, 70, 85

Continuation Committee, 4

Craig, Clarence T., 30, 67

Cunliffe-Jones, Hubert, 136

Dale, R. W., 40

Daniel, 50

Davies, R. E., quoted, 12, 52, 63

Demant, V. A., 11

"Denominational dilemma," 5

de Rougemont, Denis, 104, 105

Deuteronomy, 46, 123

Devadutt, V. E., 30

Diakonia, 130

Documents on Christian Unity: Third Series, quoted, 58

Dodd, C. H., 30, 50

Dogmatics, 22

East Harlem Protestant Parish, 104

Eastern Orthodoxy, 31, 75

Ecumenical Review, quoted, 67, 131

Edinburgh, x, 2, 3, 9, 115, 117

Egypt, 123, 124

Eliot, T. S., x, 11, 91

Enoch, 50

Episcopalian, 67

Eschatological Congregation, The, 136

Established Church, 70

Eucharist, 72

Evangelical and Reformed Church, 66, 126

Evangelization of Modern Man in Mass Society, 102

Evanston, ix, x, xi, 64, 78, 86, 96, 117, 131

Evanston: An Interpretation, quoted, xvi

Evanston Report, The, quoted, 16, 54, 79, 87, 96, 131

Ezekiel, 50

Faith and Order Commission, ix

Faith and Order Conference, 44

Faith and Order: Edinburgh 1937, quoted, 115, 117

Faith, Freedom, and the Future, quoted, 127, 128

First Assembly of the World Council of Churches, The, quoted, 117

Flew, R. Newton, quoted, 12, 52, 63, 80

Florovsky, Georges, 30

Form of the Church, The, 131; quoted, 70, 71

Forsyth, P. T., 36, 37, 70, 87, 103, 127

Fourth Gospel, 33

Free Churches, 12, 52, 68, 71, 86

Gift of Catholic Vision, The, 1

Gift of Ministry, The, quoted, 34

Great Vacuum in Christian Theology, The, 47

Grobel, Kendrick, 134

Harnack, Adolf von, 24

Hartt, Julian N., quoted, 98

Hebert, A. G., 70, 71, 72, 131

Hegelian, 95

Henley, W. E., 39

Heritage of the Reformation, The, quoted, 50, 51, 129

Hermann, Wilhelm, 23

History and the Gospel, quoted, 50

Hodgson, Leonard, quoted, 2, 9, 117

Hoover Lectures, 133

Horton, Douglas, 133

Horton, Walter M., 68, 101; quoted, 21

Idea of a Christian Society, The, quoted, 91, 92

If, 39

Independents, 71

India, Burma and Ceylon, Church of, 57

Innocent III, 35

Institutes of the Christian Religion, quoted, 51

Intellectual Slave Market, quoted, 93
Intercommunion, quoted, 118
International Missionary Council, ix, 4, 56, 92, 95, 102, 120
Invictus, 39
Isaiah, 50
Israel, 33, 45, 49, 50, 123, 124
Issues of Christian Unity, The, 76

James I, 85
Jenkins, Daniel T., 34, 40, 121; quoted, 115
Jeremiah, 32, 50
Journals, 96

Kerygma, 130
Kierkegaard, Soren, 96
Kipling, Rudyard, 39
Koinonia, 44, 62, 130
Kraemer, Hendrik, 41, 101

Lagny, M. G., quoted, 115
Lambeth, 1, 9, 12
Lausanne, 65
Lord's Supper, 43, 118, 134
Lund, 44
Luther, Martin, xvi, 51, 128
Lutheran, 21, 30, 52, 67, 105
Lyman Beecher Lectures, 37, 50, 103

Madras, 101
Man Born to Be King, The, 106
Man's Disorder and God's Design, quoted, 16
Maritain, Jacques, 11
Marsh, John, 33, 118
Martin, Hugh, quoted, x
McConnachie, J., 136
McNeill, John T., 69; quoted, 51
Methodist, 30, 66, 71, 72, 73, 85
Missionary Obligation of the Church, The, 56
Morrison, Charles Clayton, 50, 133
Moses, 123

Nagpur, 57
National Council of Churches, 66, 101, 130
National Council of Churches, Division of Home Missions, 131

Nature of the Church, The, quoted, 80
Newbigin, Lesslie, 11, 16, 129; quoted, 60
New Yorker, The, 46, 47
Nichols, James Hastings, xvi
Niebuhr, H. Richard, 1
Niebuhr, Reinhold, 11, 12, 13, 123
Niles, D. T., 96, 130
Nygren, Anders, 21, 30

Open Bible, The, quoted, 49
Orchard, R. K., 49
Oxford, x, 30

Pacific School of Religion, 102
Pauck, Wilhelm, 50, 51; quoted, 129
Paul, 32, 131, 134
Pentecost, 33
Peter, First Epistle of, 124
Philippians, Epistle to, 131, 132
Positive Preaching and the Modern Mind, quoted, 36, 103
Presbyterian, 11, 30, 66, 67, 71, 72
Promised Land, 124
Protestant, xvi, 6, 12, 42, 50, 51, 52, 62, 66, 80, 85, 86, 100, 106
Protestantism, 5, 6, 11, 37, 44, 50, 51, 84

Reader's Digest, The, 46, 47
Reformation Old and New, quoted, 99
Reformation, The, xvi, 19, 42, 50, 51, 52, 69, 114, 128
Reformed, 105, 118
Reformers, 15, 42, 50, 51, 52
Renewal and Advance, 102
Reunion of the Church, The, 11; quoted, 16, 60, 129
Reunion of the Church Through the Renewal of the Churches, 12
Revelation, x, 104
Richardson, Alan, 30; quoted, 32
Roman, 42, 105
Romans, Epistle to, 23, 24
Russian Orthodox, 30

Sacrament, 42, 43, 55, 62, 64, 80, 115, 118, 121, 134
St. Matthew, 121

Saturday Review of Literature, 92

Sayers, Dorothy, 106, 107

Schweitzer, Wolfgang, quoted, 32

Scots Confession, The, 35

Second Assembly, Message from, quoted, 54, 64

Second Assembly, World Council, xi, 16

Second World Conference on Faith and Order, The, quoted, 2, 9

South India, 9, 11, 12, 57, 59, 60, 62, 63, 74, 122, 129

South India, The Church of, quoted, 122

Strange New World within the Bible, The, 94

Temple, William, 3, 11

Theology of the New Testament, 134

Theology Today, quoted, 1, 48

Tomkins, Oliver, 3, 4, 11, 64; quoted, 111, 115

Toronto, 67

Toward a Reborn Church, quoted, 21, 68

Toward a Theology of Evangelism, quoted, 98

Towards Reunion, quoted, 87, 88

Unfinished Reformation, The, 133

Unitive Protestantism, quoted, 51, 69

Universal Church in God's Design, The, quoted, 5, 64, 65, 67

Van Dusen, Henry P., 65, 72, 76; quoted, 59

Visser 't Hooft, W. A., 5, 16; quoted, 117

Wallace, DeWitt, 47

Warren, Max, 110

Wartburg, 128

Ways of Worship, Report of Commission on, quoted, 44

Wedel, Theodore O., 47, 48

Wesley, John, 51

What Is Christianity?, 50

What Must the Church Do?, quoted, xvi

Whitby Conference, 102

White, Hugh Vernon, 102

Wholeness of the Church, The, quoted, 4, 11, 64, 111, 115

Willingen, 56

Wittenberg, 128

Word of God and the Word of Man, The, quoted, x, 24, 108

World Christianity, quoted, 59, 73

World Conference on Christian Missions, 4

World Conference on Faith and Order, 4

World Council of Churches, ix, 3, 4, 5, 10, 11, 16, 21, 28, 32, 52, 65, 67, 68, 69, 87, 91, 92, 96, 115, 118, 119, 120

World Council of Churches, Central Committee of, 67

World Council of Churches, Study Department of, xii, 10, 27, 32, 102, 104, 133

World Missionary Conference, 3

Wright, G. Ernest, 30; quoted, 104

Yale University Divinity School, 98, 101

Zwinglians, 51

Set in Linotype Electra
Format by Marguerite Swanton
Manufactured by The Haddon Craftsmen, Inc.
Published by HARPER & BROTHERS, New York